# Handbook of
# Transfusion
# Medicine

Editor: Dr Derek Norfolk

## United Kingdom Blood Services
### 5th edition

information & publishing solutions

Published by TSO and available from:

Online
www.tsoshop.co.uk

Mail, Telephone, Fax & E-mail
TSO
PO Box 29, Norwich NR3 1GN
Telephone orders/General enquiries: 0870 600 5522
Fax orders: 0870 600 5533
E-mail: customer.services@tso.co.uk
Textphone: 0870 240 3701

TSO@Blackwell and other Accredited Agents

Editor
Dr Derek Norfolk
c/o Caroline Smith
JPAC Manager
NHS Blood and Transplant
Longley Lane
SHEFFIELD
S5 7JN

Email: caroline.smith@nhsbt.nhs.uk

First published 2013

ISBN 9780117068469

Printed in the United Kingdom by The Stationery Office.

# Contents

# List of figures

# List of tables

# Preface

Although the *Handbook of Transfusion Medicine* has reached a fifth edition, its purpose remains the same – to help the many staff involved in the transfusion chain to give the right blood to the right patient at the right time (and, hopefully, for the right reason). Transfusion is a complex process that requires everyone, from senior doctors to porters and telephonists, to understand the vital role they play in safely delivering this key component of modern medicine. Training and appropriate technological and managerial support for staff is essential, and e-learning systems such as http://www.learnbloodtransfusion.org.uk are freely available. However, SHOT (Serious Hazards of Transfusion) annual reports highlight the importance of a poor knowledge of transfusion science and clinical guidelines as a cause of inappropriate and unnecessary transfusions. The handbook attempts to summarise current knowledge and best clinical practice. Wherever possible it draws upon evidence-based guidelines, especially those produced by the British Committee for Standards in Haematology (BCSH). Each chapter is now preceded by a short list of 'Essentials' – key facts extracted from the text.

We have much to congratulate ourselves about. Haemovigilance data from SHOT show that blood transfusion in the UK is very safe, with a risk of death of around 3 in 1000000 components issued. Transfusion-transmitted infections are now rare events. Lessons from blood transfusion about the importance of patient identification have improved many other areas of medical practice. But not all is well. Six of the nine deaths associated with transfusion in 2012 were linked to transfusion-associated circulatory overload (TACO), emphasising the importance of careful clinical assessment and monitoring. More than half of serious transfusion incidents are still caused by human error, especially in the identification of patients at sampling and transfusion, and each incident is accompanied by 100 near-miss events. Training and competency assessment of practitioners has been only partially effective and innovative solutions such as the use of bedside barcode scanners or transfusion checklists are slowly entering practice.

Most UK regions have seen a significant reduction in the use of red cells over the last decade, especially in surgery, but requests for platelet and plasma components continue to rise. Audits show significant variation in transfusion practice between clinical teams and poor compliance with clinical guidelines. Changing clinical behaviour is difficult, but IT-based clinician decision support systems, linked to guidelines, have real potential to improve prescribing of blood components. As we move from eminence-based to evidence-based medicine, good clinical research will be an important tool in effecting change. Since the last edition of the handbook in 2007, there has been an encouraging growth in high-quality research in transfusion medicine, including large randomised controlled trials with major implications for the safe and effective care of patients. These include the seminal CRASH-2 trial showing the benefit of a cheap and readily available antifibrinolytic treatment (tranexamic acid) in reducing mortality in major traumatic haemorrhage and studies confirming the safety of restrictive red cell transfusion policies in many surgical and critical care patients. High-quality systematic reviews of clinical trials in transfusion therapy are an increasingly valuable resource. Everyone involved in transfusion has a role in identifying clinically important questions that could be answered by further research.

Paul Glaziou, professor of evidence-based medicine at Bond University in Australia, talks about the 'hyperactive therapeutic reflex' of clinicians and the importance of 'treating the patient, not the label'. Furthermore, people increasingly want to be involved in decisions about their treatment. In transfusion medicine there is a growing emphasis on careful clinical assessment, rather than a blind reliance on laboratory tests, in making the decision to transfuse and using clinically relevant, patient-centred endpoints to assess the benefits of the transfusion. For example, reducing fatigue and improving health-related quality of life in elderly transfusion-dependent patients is more important than achieving an arbitrary target Hb level. Importantly, although guidelines outline the best evidence on which to base local policies they must always be interpreted in the light of the individual clinical situation.

Other major changes since the last edition of the handbook include:

- Reduced concern that a major epidemic of variant Creutzfeldt–Jakob disease (vCJD) will occur, although many precautions, such as the importation of all manufactured plasma products and fresh frozen plasma for patients born after 1 January 1996, remain in place. No practical vCJD screening test for blood donations has been developed.
- All UK countries have now introduced automated pre-release bacterial screening of platelet components, although the incidence of bacterial transmission had already fallen significantly following better donor arm cleaning and diversion of the first 20–30 mL of each donation.
- Implementation of the Blood Safety and Quality Regulations 2005 (BSQR) has led to the development (and inspection) of comprehensive quality systems in hospital transfusion services and the reporting of serious adverse events and reactions to the Medicines and Healthcare Products Regulatory Agency (MHRA). MHRA now works very closely with the SHOT haemovigilance scheme with the objective of improving patient safety.

Having edited this fifth edition of the handbook, I am increasingly impressed by the achievements, and fortitude, of my predecessor Dr Brian McClelland in taking the first four through to publication. Colleagues from many disciplines have kindly contributed to or reviewed sections of the handbook (see Appendix 2) but the responsibility for any of the inevitable errors and omissions is mine alone. I would like to thank the members of the JPAC Standing Advisory Committee on Clinical Transfusion Medicine for their support and advice. A special word of thanks is due to Caroline Smith for her skill and good humour in organising so many aspects of the publication process and ensuring I met (most of) the deadlines.

As well as the printed edition, the handbook will also be published in PDF and web versions that can be accessed through http://www.transfusionguidelines.org.uk. As important new information emerges, or corrections and amendments to the text are required, these will be published in the electronic versions. Transfusion medicine is changing quickly and it is important to use the up-to-date versions of evidence-based guidelines. Links to key guidelines and other online publications are inserted in the text and a list of key references and useful sources of information are given in Appendix 1.

**Derek Norfolk**
*August 2013*

# 1

**TRANSFUSION TEN
COMMANDMENTS**

# Essentials

- Is blood transfusion necessary in this patient?
- If so, ensure:
  - right blood
  - right patient
  - right time
  - right place.

1   Transfusion should only be used when the benefits outweigh the risks and there are no appropriate alternatives.

2   Results of laboratory tests are not the sole deciding factor for transfusion.

3   Transfusion decisions should be based on clinical assessment underpinned by evidence-based clinical guidelines.

4   Not all anaemic patients need transfusion (there is no universal 'transfusion trigger').

5   Discuss the risks, benefits and alternatives to transfusion with the patient and gain their consent.

6   The reason for transfusion should be documented in the patient's clinical record.

7   Timely provision of blood component support in major haemorrhage can improve outcome – good communication and team work are essential.

8   Failure to check patient identity can be fatal. Patients must wear an ID band (or equivalent) with name, date of birth and unique ID number. Confirm identity at every stage of the transfusion process. Patient identifiers on the ID band and blood pack must be identical. **Any discrepancy, DO NOT TRANSFUSE**.

9   The patient must be monitored during the transfusion.

10  Education and training underpin safe transfusion practice.

These principles (which are adapted from the NHS Blood and Transplant 'Transfusion 10 commandments' bookmark with permission) underpin safe and effective transfusion practice and form the basis for the handbook.

1 Transfusion ten commandments

# 2

## BASICS OF BLOOD GROUPS AND ANTIBODIES

# Essentials

- ABO-incompatible red cell transfusion is often fatal and its prevention is the most important step in clinical transfusion practice.
- Alloantibodies produced by exposure to blood of a different group by transfusion or pregnancy can cause transfusion reactions, haemolytic disease of the fetus and newborn (HDFN) or problems in selecting blood for regularly transfused patients.
- To prevent sensitisation and the risk of HDFN, RhD negative or Kell (K) negative girls and women of child-bearing potential should not be transfused with RhD or K positive red cells except in an emergency.
- Use of automated analysers, linked to laboratory information systems, for blood grouping and antibody screening reduces human error and is essential for the issuing of blood by electronic selection or remote issue.
- When electronic issue is not appropriate and in procedures with a high probability of requiring transfusion a maximum surgical blood ordering schedule (MSBOS) should be agreed between the surgical team and transfusion laboratory.

There are more than 300 human blood groups but only a minority cause clinically significant transfusion reactions. The two most important in clinical practice are the ABO and Rh systems.

## 2.1 Blood group antigens

Blood group antigens are molecules present on the surface of red blood cells. Some, such as the ABO groups, are also present on platelets and other tissues of the body. The genes for most blood groups have now been identified and tests based on this technology are gradually entering clinical practice.

## 2.2 Blood group antibodies

These are usually produced when an individual is exposed to blood of a different group by transfusion or pregnancy ('alloantibodies'). This is a particular problem in patients who require repeated transfusions, for conditions such as thalassaemia or sickle cell disease, and can cause difficulties in providing fully compatible blood if the patient is immunised to several different groups (see Chapter 8). Some antibodies react with red cells around the normal body temperature of 37°C (warm antibodies). Others are only active at lower temperatures (cold antibodies) and do not usually cause clinical problems although they may be picked up on laboratory testing.

## 2.3 Testing for red cell antigens and antibodies in the laboratory

The ABO blood group system was the first to be discovered because anti-A and anti-B are mainly of the IgM immunoglobulin class and cause visible agglutination of group A or B red cells in laboratory mixing tests. Antibodies to ABO antigens are naturally occurring and are found in everyone after the first 3 months of life. Many other blood group antibodies, such

**2 Basics of blood groups and antibodies**

7

as those against the Rh antigens, are smaller IgG molecules and do not directly cause agglutination of red cells. These 'incomplete antibodies' can be detected by the antiglobulin test (Coombs' test) using antibodies to human IgG, IgM or complement components ('antiglobulin') raised in laboratory animals. The direct antiglobulin test (DAT) is used to detect antibodies present on circulating red cells, as in autoimmune haemolytic anaemia or after mismatch blood transfusion. Blood group antibodies in plasma are demonstrated by the indirect antiglobulin test (IAT). Nearly all clinically significant red cell antibodies can be detected by an IAT antibody screen carried out at 37°C (see section 2.7).

# 2.4   The ABO system

There are four main blood groups: A, B, AB and O. All normal individuals have antibodies to the A or B antigens that are not present on their own red cells (Table 2.1). The frequency of ABO groups varies in different ethnic populations and this must be taken into account when recruiting representative blood donor panels. For example, people of Asian origin have a higher frequency of group B than white Europeans. Individuals of blood group O are sometimes known as universal donors as their red cells have no A or B antigens. However, their plasma does contain anti-A and anti-B that, if present in high titre, has the potential to haemolyse the red cells of certain non-group O recipients (see below).

**Table 2.1  Distribution of ABO blood groups and antibodies**

| Blood group | Antigens on red cells | Antibodies in plasma | UK blood donors |
|---|---|---|---|
| O | none | anti-A and anti-B | 47% |
| A | A | anti-B | 42% |
| B | B | anti-A | 8% |
| AB | A and B | none | 3% |

## 2.4.1   Transfusion reactions due to ABO incompatibility

ABO-incompatible red cell transfusion is often fatal and its prevention is the most important step in clinical transfusion practice (Chapter 5). Anti-A and/or anti-B in the recipient's plasma binds to the transfused cells and activates the complement pathway, leading to destruction of the transfused red cells (intravascular haemolysis) and the release of inflammatory cytokines that can cause shock, renal failure and disseminated intravascular coagulation (DIC). The accidental transfusion of ABO-incompatible blood is now classified as a 'never event' by the UK Departments of Health.

Transfusion of ABO-incompatible plasma containing anti-A or anti-B, usually from a group O donor, can cause haemolysis of the recipient's red cells, especially in neonates and small infants. Red cells stored in saline, adenine, glucose and mannitol (SAG-M) additive solution (see Chapter 3) contain less than 20 mL of residual plasma so the risk of haemolytic reactions is very low. Group O red cell components for intrauterine transfusion, neonatal exchange transfusion or large-volume transfusion of infants are screened to exclude those with high-titre anti-A or anti-B. Group O plasma-rich blood components such as fresh frozen plasma (FFP) or platelet concentrates should not be given to patients of group A, B or AB if ABO-compatible components are readily available (Table 2.2).

Cryoprecipitate contains very little immunoglobulin and has never been reported to cause significant haemolysis. In view of the importance of making AB plasma readily available, AB cryoprecipitate manufacture and availability is a low priority for the UK Blood Services.

**Table 2.2 Choice of group of red cells, platelets, fresh frozen plasma (FFP) and cryoprecipitate according to recipient's ABO group**

| Patient's ABO group | Red cells | Platelets[a] | Fresh frozen plasma (FFP)[b] | Cryoprecipitate |
|---|---|---|---|---|
| **O** | | | | |
| First choice | O | O | O | O |
| Second choice | | A | A or B | A or B |
| Third choice | | | AB | |
| **A** | | | | |
| First choice | A | A | A | A |
| Second choice | O[c] | O[d] | AB | O or B |
| Third choice | | | B[d] | |
| **B** | | | | |
| First choice | B | A[d] | B | B |
| Second choice | O[c] | O[d] | AB | O or A |
| Third choice | | | A[d] | |
| **AB** | | | | |
| First choice | AB | A[d] | AB | AB |
| Second choice | A or B | O[d] | A[d] | A or B |
| Third choice | O[c] | | B[d] | O |

[a] Group B or AB platelets are not routinely available

[b] Group AB FFP is often in short supply

[c] Screening for high-titre anti-A and anti-B is not required if plasma-depleted group O red cells in SAG-M are used

[d] Tested and negative for high-titre anti-A and anti-B

# 2.5   The Rh system

There are five main Rh antigens on red cells for which individuals can be positive or negative: C/c, D and E/e. RhD is the most important in clinical practice. Around 85% of white Northern Europeans are RhD positive, rising to virtually 100% of people of Chinese origin. Antibodies to RhD (anti-D) are only present in RhD negative individuals who have been transfused with RhD positive red cells or in RhD negative women who have been pregnant with an RhD positive baby. IgG anti-D antibodies can cause acute or delayed haemolytic transfusion reactions when RhD positive red cells are transfused and may cause haemolytic disease of the fetus and newborn (HDFN – see Chapter 9). It is important to avoid exposing RhD negative girls and women of child-bearing potential to RhD positive red cell transfusions except in extreme emergencies when no other group is immediately available.

## 2.6   Other clinically important blood group systems

Alloantibodies to the Kidd (Jk) system are an important cause of delayed haemolytic transfusion reactions (see Chapter 5). Kell (anti-K) alloantibodies can cause HDFN and it is important to avoid transfusing K positive red cells to K negative girls and women of child-bearing potential. Before red cell transfusion, the plasma of recipients is screened for clinically important red cell alloantibodies so that compatible blood can be selected.

## 2.7   Compatibility procedures in the hospital transfusion laboratory

### 2.7.1   Group and screen

The patient's pre-transfusion blood sample is tested to determine the ABO and RhD groups and the plasma is screened for the presence of red cell alloantibodies capable of causing transfusion reactions. Antibody screening is performed using a panel of red cells that contains examples of the clinically important blood groups most often seen in practice. Blood units of a compatible ABO and Rh group, negative for any blood group alloantibodies detected, can then be selected from the blood bank, taking into account any special requirements on the transfusion request such as irradiated or cytomegalovirus (CMV) negative components.

Almost all hospital laboratories carry out blood grouping and antibody screening using automated analysers with computer control of specimen identification and result allocation. This is much safer than traditional manual techniques and eliminates most transcription and interpretation errors. ABO grouping is the single most important test performed on pre-transfusion samples and the sensitivity and security of testing systems must never be compromised. Robust identification procedures outside the laboratory at patient blood sampling, collection of blood from the blood bank and administration of blood at the bedside are vital (see Chapter 4). The current British Committee for Standards in Haematology (BCSH) guideline for pre-transfusion compatibility procedures (2012) recommends that a second sample should be requested for confirmation of the ABO group of a first-time transfused patient provided this does not impede the delivery of urgent red cells or components (http://www.bcshguidelines.com).

### 2.7.2   Compatibility testing

Traditionally, the final step in providing safe blood is to carry out a serological crossmatch between the patient's plasma and a sample of red cells from the units of blood selected for transfusion. This is performed by the IAT method at 37°C, looking for evidence of a reaction that would indicate incompatibility.

### 2.7.3    Electronic issue

This is sometimes known as computer crossmatching. Most hospitals now issue the majority of blood by this safe and rapid technique. It relies on the fact that if the patient's ABO and RhD groups are reliably established, and a sensitive antibody screen is negative, the possibility of issuing incompatible blood is negligible. The laboratory computer can identify all compatible units in the blood bank inventory without the need for further testing. National guidelines require the use of automated testing systems interfaced with laboratory information systems before electronic selection is used and all results must be transmitted electronically to remove human error. Electronic issue **should not** be used:

- If the patient's plasma contains, or has been known to contain, red cell alloantibodies of clinical significance
- If the antibody screen is positive
- If the patient has had an ABO-incompatible marrow or haemopoietic stem cell transplant
- If the patient has had an ABO-incompatible solid organ transplant in the last 3 months
- For neonates or fetuses, if the mother has an IgG red cell antibody present in her plasma.

### 2.7.4    Blood for planned procedures

Many operations rarely need transfusion. As long as the laboratory can provide components quickly in an emergency, there is no need to reserve blood units in the blood bank. Group and screen and electronic issue are now widely used in this situation and allow more efficient use of blood stocks and laboratory scientist time.

Patients undergoing planned procedures that may require transfusion, such as major surgery, ideally have samples for group and screen taken at preadmission clinics. Problems in providing compatible blood are then identified before admission to hospital. There is a (usually small) risk that the patient may develop new blood group alloantibodies between the time of initial testing and the date of operation, especially if they have recently been transfused or become pregnant. Having reviewed current evidence, the BCSH guidelines for pre-transfusion compatibility procedures (Milkins *et al.*, 2012) made the following pragmatic recommendations for timing of pre-transfusion blood samples:

- Testing should be performed on samples collected no more than 3 days in advance of the transfusion when the patient has been transfused or become pregnant within the preceding 3 months.
- An extension to 7 days may be considered for regularly/frequently transfused patients with no alloantibodies and pregnant women with no significant alloantibodies who need to have blood standing by for a potential obstetric emergency such as placenta praevia.

Remote issue of compatible blood components from satellite blood refrigerators electronically linked to the laboratory computer system allows safe and efficient provision of blood when the transfusion laboratory and operating theatres are on different hospital sites. Successful adoption of this approach requires close collaboration with the clinical team and clear local guidelines and policies.

When electronic issue is not available or appropriate and in procedures with a high probability of requiring transfusion a maximum surgical blood ordering schedule (MSBOS) should be agreed between the surgical team and transfusion laboratory. This specifies how many blood units will be routinely reserved (in the blood bank or satellite refrigerator) for standard procedures, based on audits of local practice. When developing an MSBOS it is usual to aim for a crossmatched to transfused ratio of no more than 3:1 and actual blood use should be audited and reviewed at regular intervals.

2 Basics of blood groups and antibodies

# 3

## PROVIDING
## SAFE BLOOD

## Essentials

- Unpaid volunteers, donating regularly, are key to the provision of safe and sufficient blood for transfusion.
- 17 to 65 year olds can enrol as first-time blood donors and there is no upper age limit for regular donors (subject to an annual health check).
- To ensure the safety of the donor and recipient, a medical questionnaire covering health, lifestyle, travel history, medical history and medication is completed before each donation.
- The minimum mandatory infection screen on all donations is for hepatitis B and C, HIV, HTLV and syphilis, and extra tests are performed as required.
- The risk of transmission of prion diseases such as variant Creutzfeldt–Jakob disease (vCJD) is reduced by excluding at-risk donors (including recipients of a blood transfusion or tissue/organ transplant since 1980), removing white cells from donations (leucodepletion), importing plasma derivatives from countries with a low risk of vCJD and providing imported, virus-inactivated fresh frozen plasma (FFP) for patients born on or after 1 January 1996.
- Donations are routinely ABO and RhD typed and screened for clinically important blood group antibodies.
- Modern transfusion practice is based on the use of blood components rather than whole blood donations.
- Plasma derivatives are licensed medicines and include albumin solutions, coagulation factor concentrates and immunoglobulins.

Blood transfusion in the UK is now very safe indeed and most serious adverse events originate in the hospital rather than the blood transfusion centre (see Chapter 5). However, ensuring a safe and effective blood supply remains essential. This requires a combination of high-quality donor recruitment and selection, infection screening, serological testing and blood component production (followed by rational clinical use). The four UK Blood Services – NHS Blood and Transplant, Northern Ireland Blood Transfusion Service, Scottish National Blood Transfusion Service and Welsh Blood Service – maintain common standards for blood donation, testing and blood products. The Joint UKBTS Professional Advisory Committee (JPAC) is responsible for producing the *Guidelines for the Blood Transfusion Services in the UK*, often known as the Red Book (http://www.transfusionguidelines.org.uk/). In 2011 the UK Blood Services issued 2.1 million units of red cells, 300 000 platelet doses, 288 000 units of fresh frozen plasma and 126 000 units of cryoprecipitate.

## 3.1 Blood donation

Unpaid volunteers who donate on a regular basis are a crucial element in the provision of a safe and reliable supply of blood. Many studies show that altruistic donors have a lower prevalence of transfusion-transmissible infections.

The minimum age for donation is 17 years. There is no upper age limit for regular donors, although they are subject to annual health review after their 66th birthday. The upper age limit for first-time donors is 65 years. The minimum body weight for blood donation is 50 kg (7 st 12 lb). Only 5% of eligible people are regular blood donors and the Blood Services put much effort into improving recruitment, especially of donors from minority ethnic groups.

3 Providing safe blood

### 3.1.1 Donor eligibility

Donors answer a series of questions before each donation relating to their health, lifestyle, travel history, medical history and medication. This is to ensure the safety of both the donor and recipients. Donor exclusion and deferral criteria are regularly reviewed in the light of scientific knowledge. For example, there have been recent significant changes to the eligibility of 'men who have sex with men' (MSM) to donate blood in the UK (see Chapter 5). Up-to-date eligibility criteria are given in the Red Book (http://www.transfusionguidelines.org.uk/).

### 3.1.2 Frequency of donation

The normal interval between whole blood donations is 16 weeks (minimum 12 weeks) but no more than three donations a year are collected from female donors because of their more precarious iron status. Donors undergo a screening test for anaemia, usually the copper sulphate flotation test on a finger prick sample. The minimum pre-donation Hb concentration is 125 g/L for female donors and 135 g/L for males.

Donors giving double red cell donations by apheresis must have a pre-donation Hb concentration of 140 g/L and the minimum interval between donations is 26 weeks.

Donors can give platelets or plasma by apheresis on a cell separator with a maximum of 24 procedures in 12 months. The minimum interval between donations is 2 weeks and plasma donors are limited to 15 litres a year.

### 3.1.3 Genetic haemochromatosis

Donors with this common genetic condition, which causes increased iron absorption from the diet, are eligible to become blood donors if they meet all the other medical selection and age criteria. Regular blood donation can be part of their maintenance treatment schedule to prevent iron overload.

## 3.2 Tests on blood donations

### 3.2.1 Screening for infectious agents

At each donation, the following mandatory tests are performed:

- Hepatitis B – HBsAg
- Human immunodeficiency virus – anti-HIV 1 and 2 and HIV NAT (nucleic acid testing)
- Hepatitis C – anti-HCV and HCV NAT
- Human T-cell lymphotropic virus – anti-HTLV I and II
- Syphilis – syphilis antibodies.

Some donations are tested for cytomegalovirus (CMV) antibodies to provide CMV negative blood for patients with certain types of impaired immunity (see Chapter 5).

Additional tests, performed in special circumstances, include:

- Malarial antibodies
- West Nile Virus antibodies
- *Trypanosoma cruzi* antibodies.

### 3.2.2 Precautions to reduce the transfusion transmission of prion-associated diseases

These include variant Creutzfeldt–Jakob disease (vCJD – caused by the same agent as bovine spongiform encephalopathy (BSE) in cattle – 'mad cow disease') and sporadic or inherited CJD. The following are permanently deferred from blood donation:

- Persons who have received a blood transfusion or tissue/organ transplant from a donor since 1980
- Anyone who has received human pituitary-derived hormones, grafts of human dura mater or cornea, sclera or other ocular tissue
- Members of a family at risk of inherited prion diseases
- Persons notified that they may be at increased risk of vCJD due to possible exposure to an infected individual by surgical instruments, blood product transfusion or transplant of tissues or organs
- Persons notified that they may be at increased risk because a recipient of their blood or tissues has developed a prion-related disorder.

More information, including the latest data on transfusion-transmitted vCJD, can be obtained from the National CJD Research and Surveillance Unit (http://www.cjd.ed.ac.uk/index.html).

### 3.2.3 Blood groups and blood group antibodies

Every donation is tested to determine the ABO and RhD group of the red cells and the plasma is screened to detect the most common blood group antibodies that might cause problems in a recipient. Some donations are tested for a wider range of clinically significant blood groups (extended phenotyping) to allow closer matching and reduce the development of alloantibodies in patients who need long-term red cell transfusion support (see Chapter 8). Blood for neonatal or intrauterine use has a more extensive antibody screen (see Chapter 10).

Some group O donations are screened for high levels of anti-A and anti-B antibodies to reduce the risk of haemolytic reactions when group O plasma, platelets or other components containing a large amount of plasma (e.g. red cells for intrauterine or neonatal exchange transfusion) are transfused to group A, B or AB patients, especially neonates and infants.

### 3.2.4 Molecular blood group testing

The genes for most human blood groups have now been identified. Currently only a limited number of patients undergo genotyping. These include recently transfused patients whose blood group is uncertain and fetuses that require typing to define the risk from maternal antibodies. Routine DNA testing/genotyping using rapid automated technology is likely to enter blood service and hospital laboratory practice in the next decade.

## 3.3 Blood products

These are classified as blood components prepared in the blood transfusion centre (red cells, platelets, fresh frozen plasma and cryoprecipitate) or plasma derivatives manufactured from pooled plasma donations in plasma fractionation centres (such as albumin, coagulation factors and immunoglobulins). Plasma derivatives are covered by the Medicines Act and, like any other drug, must be prescribed by a licensed practitioner. Since 1999, as a vCJD risk-reduction measure, all plasma derivatives used in the UK are manufactured using donations from countries with a low risk of vCJD.

3 Providing safe blood

### 3.3.1 Blood components

Whole blood is now rarely used for transfusion. Blood component therapy makes clinical sense as most patients require a specific element of blood, such as red cells or platelets, and the dose can then be optimised. Each component is stored under ideal conditions (e.g. red cells must be refrigerated, platelets must not) and the use of precious blood donations becomes more efficient. The use of blood components in clinical practice is covered in Chapters 7 to 10.

The process of producing blood components and plasma derivatives is summarised in Figure 3.1.

### 3.3.2 Labelling of blood components

#### 3.3.2.1 Blood component labels

The content of blood pack labels attached at the transfusion centre is prescribed by the Blood Safety and Quality Regulations 2005 (BSQR). Key information is present in both eye-readable and barcoded form and allows the donor origin (via a unique donation number) and processing steps of the product to be traced as well as indicating the blood group, any special requirements (such as CMV negative or irradiated), expiry date and storage conditions. Work is in progress to review the content of blood component labels and improve their clarity. Up-to-date information is available in the *Guidelines for the Blood Transfusion Services in the UK* (http://www.transfusionguidelines.org.uk).

#### 3.3.2.2 Blood compatibility labels

These are attached to the pack in the hospital transfusion laboratory and uniquely identify the patient for whom the component has been selected. At the final bedside check, the donation number and other details on the compatibility label must match those on the blood pack label and the patient details must exactly match those on the recipient's ID band (see Chapter 4 for detailed discussion of safe blood administration).

#### 3.3.2.3 Specifications of blood components

Whole blood donations of 405–495 mL (mean 470 mL) are collected into 63 mL of citrate phosphate dextrose (CPD) anticoagulant.

All blood donations are filtered to remove white blood cells (pre-storage leucodepletion) to leave $<1\times10^6$ leucocytes in the pack. This was introduced in 1998 as a vCJD risk-reduction measure but also reduces the incidence of febrile transfusion reactions and alloimmunisation to white cell (including HLA) antigens.

Indicative contents of commonly available components are noted below, based on quality assurance data from NHS Blood and Transplant (see http://www.blood.co.uk/hospitals/products for more detail and an up-to-date compendium). Blood components for neonates and intrauterine transfusion are discussed in Chapter 10.

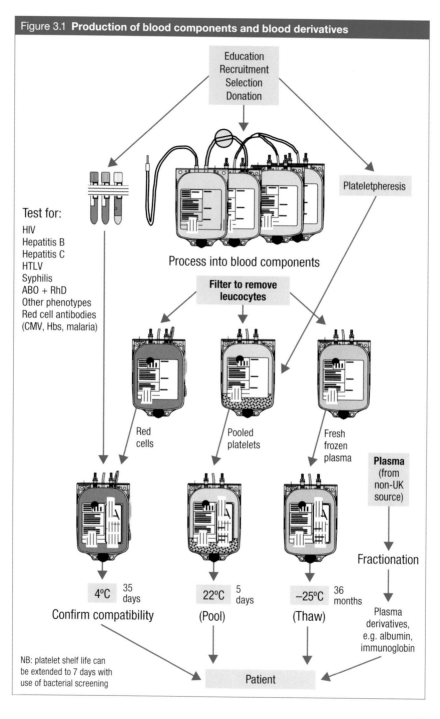

Figure 3.1 **Production of blood components and blood derivatives**

Education
Recruitment
Selection
Donation

Plateletpheresis

Test for:
HIV
Hepatitis B
Hepatitis C
HTLV
Syphilis
ABO + RhD
Other phenotypes
Red cell antibodies
(CMV, Hbs, malaria)

Process into blood components

**Filter to remove leucocytes**

Red cells

Pooled platelets

Fresh frozen plasma

**Plasma** (from non-UK source)

4°C — 35 days

22°C — 5 days

−25°C — 36 months

Fractionation

Confirm compatibility

(Pool)

(Thaw)

Plasma derivatives, e.g. albumin, immunoglobin

NB: platelet shelf life can be extended to 7 days with use of bacterial screening

Patient

## Red cells

These are used to restore oxygen carrying capacity in patients with anaemia or blood loss where alternative treatments are ineffective or inappropriate. They must be ABO compatible with the recipient (see Table 2.2). Clinical indications for red cell transfusion are discussed in Chapters 7 to 10.

### Red cells in additive solution

In red cells in additive solution (Table 3.1) the majority of plasma is removed and replaced by 100 mL saline, adenine, glucose and mannitol additive solution (SAG-M).

**Table 3.1  Red cells in additive solution**

| | |
|---|---|
| Volume (mL) | 220–340 |
| Haematocrit (L/L) | 0.5–0.7 |
| Haemoglobin content (g) | >40 (in more than 75% of units tested) |
| Residual plasma (mL) | 5–30 |
| Storage temperature | 2–6°C |
| Shelf life | Up to 35 days from donation |

### Irradiated red cells

Irradiated red cells are indicated for patients at risk of transfusion-associated graft-versus-host disease (TA-GvHD – see Chapter 8). The component must be irradiated by gamma or X-rays within 14 days of donation and it then has a shelf life of 14 days from irradiation.

### Washed red cells

Indicated for patients with recurrent or severe allergic or febrile reactions to red cells, and severely IgA-deficient patients with anti-IgA antibodies for whom red cells from an IgA-deficient donor are not available (see Chapter 5). They are produced either manually (24-hour shelf life) or by a closed, automated system in which the red cells are sequentially washed to remove most of the plasma (<0.5 g residual plasma per unit) and then resuspended in 100 mL SAG-M (shelf life 14 days from washing).

## Platelets

Platelet transfusion is indicated for the treatment or prevention of bleeding in patients with a low platelet count (thrombocytopenia) or platelet dysfunction. An adult therapeutic dose (ATD) of platelets is >240×10$^9$ per transfusion.

Platelets have ABO antigens on their surface and may have reduced survival if transfused to an ABO-incompatible recipient, although this is not usually clinically significant. They are usually only available in groups O, A or B, with only a small number of group AB platelets produced.

Anti-A or anti-B antibodies in the plasma of platelet components may rarely cause haemolysis of the recipient's red cells, especially in babies and small children. Group O platelets should ideally only be given to group O recipients. Selection of platelets for patients of other ABO groups is summarised in Table 3.2. RhD negative platelet concentrates should be given to RhD negative patients where possible, especially to RhD negative women of child-bearing potential. When RhD-incompatible platelets have to be given, administration of anti-D immunoglobulin may prevent immunisation.

Platelets are produced in two ways (see Tables 3.2 and 3.3):

■ Whole blood donations are centrifuged and the buffy coats (between the red cell and plasma layers) from four donations are pooled in the plasma of one of the donors (male, to reduce the risk of transfusion-related acute lung injury (TRALI) – see Chapter 5).
■ An ATD of platelets is obtained from a single donor by apheresis (donors may give two or three ATDs at a single session).

The UK Blood Services aim to provide more than 80% of platelet doses by apheresis to reduce the exposure of patients to multiple donors (a vCJD risk-reduction measure).

Platelets are stored in temperature-controlled incubators (20–24°C) with constant agitation (refrigerated platelets are rapidly removed from the circulation). The recent introduction of automated bacterial screening has allowed some Blood Services to extend the shelf life from 5 to 7 days after donation.

**Table 3.2 Platelets from pooled buffy coats**

| | |
|---|---|
| Number of donors per pack | 4 |
| Mean volume (mL) | 300 |
| Mean platelets ($\times 10^9$ per unit) | 308 (range 165–500) |
| Anticoagulant | CPD |
| Storage | 20–24°C with agitation |
| Shelf life | 5 days (7 days if bacterial screening) |

**Table 3.3 Platelets from apheresis donation**

| | |
|---|---|
| Number of donors per pack | 1 |
| Mean volume (mL) | 199 |
| Mean platelets ($\times 10^9$ per unit) | 280 (range 165–510) |
| Anticoagulant | Acid citrate dextrose |
| Storage | 20–24°C with agitation |
| Shelf life | 5 days (7 days if bacterial screening) |

*Irradiated platelets*
Platelets may be irradiated to prevent TA-GvHD in susceptible patients. They retain their normal shelf life.

*Platelets in additive solution*
After 'washing' to remove most of the plasma the platelets are resuspended in 200 mL of platelet additive solution (PAS). This component is indicated for patients with recurrent severe allergic or febrile reactions to standard platelet transfusions. The shelf life is reduced to 24 hours after preparation and they must be ordered specially from the Blood Service. Some platelets are lost in the washing process and the component still contains around 10 mL residual plasma.

3 Providing safe blood

*Human leucocyte antigen (HLA)-selected platelets*

Indicated for patients refractory to random platelet components because of the development of HLA antibodies after previous transfusions (see Chapter 9). The Blood Services maintain a panel of HLA-typed platelet donors who donate by apheresis. The platelets are irradiated before issue to prevent TA-GvHD.

*Human platelet antigen (HPA)-selected platelets*

HPA-1a/5b negative platelets are kept in limited numbers at strategically placed stock-holding units in the UK and are used for babies with neonatal alloimmune thrombocytopenia (NAIT) (see Chapter 10).

## Plasma

Plasma is obtained from whole blood donations or component donation by apheresis. Only male donors are used to reduce the risk of TRALI. The UK Departments of Health recommend that patients born on or after 1 January 1996 should only receive plasma sourced from countries with a low risk of vCJD. Imported plasma is treated with a pathogen reduction process, such as methylene blue or solvent detergent treatment, to reduce the risk of viral transmission.

Plasma components of the same ABO group should be transfused to patients wherever possible. If ABO-identical plasma is not available, the selection criteria given in Table 2.2 are recommended. Plasma components do not need to be matched for RhD group as they contain no red cells or red cell stroma. They do not cause TA-GvHD and irradiation is not required.

*Fresh frozen plasma (FFP)*

Plasma is frozen soon after collection to maintain the activity of blood-clotting factors. It can be stored for up to 36 months at −25°C or below. Standard UK FFP is issued as single-donor packs which must be thawed before use, usually in a purpose-designed waterbath. Thawed units of FFP can be stored for up to 24 hours at 4°C before transfusion. Clotting factor levels vary widely between normal healthy donors and this variability is reflected in the concentrations found in individual packs of FFP.

FFP (see Table 3.4) is indicated for the treatment of patients with bleeding due to multiple clotting factor deficiencies such as disseminated intravascular coagulation (DIC). It may also be used in patients with inherited clotting factor deficiencies (e.g. Factor V deficiency) where a clotting factor concentrate is not yet available. The recommended dose is 12–15 mL/kg (minimum of four units in a 70 kg adult). However, much larger doses may be needed to produce 'therapeutic' levels of coagulation factors and volume overload is a significant clinical problem. FFP is no longer indicated for the reversal of warfarin, as a specific and effective antidote is available (prothrombin complex). FFP carries a significant risk of severe allergic reactions (see Chapter 5) and should not be used as a plasma volume expander.

## Table 3.4 Fresh frozen plasma

| | |
|---|---|
| Number of donor exposures per pack | 1 |
| Mean volume (mL) | 274 |
| Mean Factor VIIIc (IU/mL) | 0.83 (specification >0.7) |
| Anticoagulant | CPD |
| Storage | <−25°C |
| Shelf life | 36 months (24 hours at 4°C after thawing) |

*Pathogen-inactivated fresh frozen plasma*

Solvent detergent treated FFP (SD-FFP) is available as a licensed medicinal product (Octaplas®, Table 3.5). It is prepared from pools with a maximum of 1520 donations and the SD process inactivates bacteria and most encapsulated viruses, including hepatitis B and C and HIV. Donations are sourced from countries with a low risk of vCJD and a prion-reduced version, Octaplas LG®, is now licensed in the UK. The pooling process leads to more standardised concentrations of clotting factors in each pack and probably explains the significantly reduced incidence of severe allergic reactions and TRALI in haemovigilance reports. SD treatment reduces the concentration of fibrinogen and Factor VIIIc by 15–20%, but levels remain within the defined specification. Levels of Protein S, an anticoagulant factor, are around 30% lower and this may be important in patients with an increased risk of thromboembolism. UK guidelines recommend imported SD-FFP for plasma exchange in patients with thrombotic thrombocytopenic purpura (TTP – see Chapter 11).

**Table 3.5  Solvent detergent plasma (Octaplas®)**

| Number of donor exposures per pack | Maximum 1520 donors per batch |
|---|---|
| Volume (mL) | 200 (standardised) |
| Mean Factor VIIIc (IU/mL) | 0.8 (specification >0.5) |
| Mean fibrinogen (mg/mL) | 2.6 (range 1.5–4.0) |
| Anticoagulant | Sodium citrate |
| Storage | <−18°C |
| Shelf life | 4 years (transfuse immediately after thawing) |

Based on data from Octapharma AG (http://www.octapharma.co.uk)

Methylene blue treated FFP (MB-FFP) is a single-donor pathogen-reduced component available through the UK Blood Services. The process inactivates encapsulated viruses and bacteria. In the UK, the methylene blue process is used to treat packs of FFP imported from low vCJD risk countries, providing a single-donor component that is preferred by some neonatologists and paediatricians. MB-FFP has a reduced activity of fibrinogen and Factor VIII. The clinical significance of this is uncertain, although some studies in cardiac surgery have suggested the need for bigger transfusions to achieve the same therapeutic effect. Like all single-donor FFP components, the content of clotting factors varies between individual packs.

*Cryoprecipitate*

Cryoprecipitate (Table 3.6) is made by thawing UK donor FFP at 4°C, producing a cryoglobulin rich in fibrinogen, Factor VIII and von Willebrand factor. It was developed as a treatment for haemophilia but this use has now been replaced by Factor VIII concentrate. Cryoprecipitate is mainly used as a more concentrated, hence lower volume for infusion, source of fibrinogen than FFP. It is available from the Blood Services as single-donor packs or as pools of five donations. The recommended adult therapeutic dose is two pools of five units (or one unit per 5–10 kg body weight), which will typically raise the plasma fibrinogen by about 1 g/L. Cryoprecipitate produced from imported MB-FFP is now available. Because of a lower concentration of fibrinogen, pools of six donations are issued.

3 Providing safe blood

### Table 3.6 Cryoprecipitate

| | Cryoprecipitate packs | Cryoprecipitate pools |
|---|---|---|
| Number of donors | 1 | 5 |
| Mean volume (mL) | 43 | 189 |
| Fibrinogen (mg/pack) | 396 (specification >140) | 1552 (specification >700) |
| Factor VIIIc (IU/pack) | 105 (specification >70) | 454 (specification >350) |
| Storage | <−25°C | <−25°C |
| Shelf life | 36 months (use within 4 hours of thawing, do not refrigerate) | 36 months (use within 4 hours of thawing, do not refrigerate) |

## Granulocytes

Although their clinical effectiveness is controversial, transfusion of granulocytes (neutrophils – phagocytic white blood cells) may be indicated in patients with life-threatening soft tissue or organ infection with bacteria or fungi and low neutrophil counts, usually in the setting of severe, prolonged neutropenia after cytotoxic chemotherapy.

There are two main granulocyte-rich components available: buffy coats derived from whole blood donations and granulocytes collected by apheresis from individual donors. Because of contaminating red cells, granulocyte components must be ABO and RhD compatible and crossmatched with the recipient. They are irradiated before issue to prevent TA-GvHD. Daily transfusions are given, with monitoring of response, until recovery of bone marrow function.

### Individual buffy coats

These buffy coats (Table 3.7) contain large numbers of red cells and the Hb/haematocrit of the recipient must be monitored. Usefully, the high platelet content may reduce the need for platelet transfusions. The recommended dose is ten buffy coats daily for adults (10–20 mL/kg for smaller children and infants).

### Table 3.7 Buffy coat (granulocytes)

| | |
|---|---|
| Mean volume per pack (mL) | 60 (10 packs = 600 mL) |
| Mean granulocytes (×10$^9$/pack) | 1.0 (10 packs = 1×10$^{10}$) |
| Haematocrit (L/L) | 0.45 |
| Platelets (×10$^9$/pack) | 70 |
| Storage | 20–24°C |
| Shelf life | To midnight on day of collection |

### Pooled buffy coats (granulocytes pooled buffy coat derived in additive solution and plasma)

This component (see Table 3.8) was introduced in the UK in 2012. Although the manufacturing process is more complicated, it has the advantages of lower volume, less red cell and plasma contamination and resuspension in male donor plasma and additive solution to reduce the risk of TRALI. The dose is two packs (20 donations) for an adult and 10–20 mL/kg for children.

### Table 3.8 Granulocytes pooled buffy coat derived in additive solution and plasma

| | |
|---|---|
| Mean volume per pack (mL) | 207 (175–250) mL |
| Mean granulocytes (×10¹⁰/pack) | 1.0 (1×10¹⁰) |
| Haematocrit (L/L) | 0.15 |
| Platelets (×10⁹/pack) | 499 (equivalent to 2.5 adult transfusion doses) |
| Storage | 20–24°C (**not** agitated) |
| Shelf life | To midnight on day following collection |

#### Apheresis granulocytes

The collection of a therapeutic dose of apheresis granulocytes (Table 3.9) requires the donor to be pre-treated with steroids and/or injections of granulocyte colony stimulating factor (G-CSF). Hence, their collection is restricted to directed donors (usually a relative) for an individual patient, rather than UK Blood Service volunteer donors, and the component is only available in certain clinical centres.

### Table 3.9 Apheresis granulocytes

| | |
|---|---|
| Mean volume per unit (mL) | 312 |
| Granulocytes per unit | >1×10¹⁰ |
| Haematocrit (L/L) | 0.23 |
| Platelets (×10⁹ per unit) | 111 |
| Storage | 20–24°C |
| Shelf life | 24 hours from collection |

## Plasma derivatives

These are licensed medicinal products manufactured from human plasma donations. Some of the main products used in hospital practice are listed below but the reader is referred to the British National Formulary (BNF – http://bnf.org/bnf) and the individual Summary of Product Characteristics for more detailed information about formulation and clinical indications. Although these products are manufactured from large donor pools, sometimes thousands of donations, all now undergo multiple pathogen inactivation steps to eradicate transfusion-transmitted viruses. Since 1999, all plasma derivatives used in the UK are derived from imported plasma (a vCJD risk-reduction measure).

#### Human albumin solution

Human albumin solution (HAS) contains no clotting factors or blood group antibodies and crossmatching is not required. The clinical indications for HAS are controversial. Crystalloid solutions or synthetic colloidal plasma substitutes are alternatives for use as plasma expanders in acute blood or plasma loss. HAS should not be used to 'correct' the low serum albumin level often associated with acute or chronic illness. Side effects include occasional severe hypersensitivity reactions. HAS is available in two forms:

- Isotonic solutions (4.5 and 5.0% in volumes of 50 to 500 mL): Often used to replace subacute plasma volume loss caused by burns, pancreatitis or trauma, and as a replacement fluid in plasma exchange.

3 Providing safe blood

25

- Concentrated solutions (20% in volumes of 50 and 100 mL): Indications may include initiating diuresis in hypoalbuminaemic patients with liver cirrhosis or nephrotic syndrome, removal of large volumes of ascites in patients with portal hypertension and to assist the reduction of high bilirubin levels by exchange transfusion in the newborn (unconjugated bilirubin binds to albumin).

### Clotting factor concentrates

Single-factor concentrates are available for the treatment of most inherited coagulation deficiencies except Factor V and Factor II (prothrombin). Most patients in the UK with severe haemophilia A are now treated with recombinant Factor VIIIc, which carries no risk of viral or prion transmission.

Fibrinogen concentrate (Factor I) is, at present, only licensed in the UK for the treatment of congenital hypofibrinogenaemia but there is encouraging international experience of its effectiveness in the much more common setting of acquired hypofibrinogenaemia (e.g. DIC, traumatic haemorrhage, massive transfusion). Many coagulation experts believe that it will replace the use of cryoprecipitate for this purpose in view of its ease of administration, convenience of storage and standardised fibrinogen content.

Prothrombin complex concentrate (PCC) contains Factors II, VII, IX and X. It has replaced FFP as the recommended treatment for rapid reversal of warfarin overdose, with elevated international normalised ratio (INR) and severe bleeding, in view of its superior efficacy, ease of administration and lower risk of severe allergic reactions or fluid overload. Modern formulations of PCC do not contain activated clotting factors and have a low risk of causing thrombotic complications. PCC may also be used to treat bleeding due to the coagulopathy associated with liver disease. The dose for reversal of warfarin is 25–50 IU/kg.

### Immunoglobulin solutions

These are manufactured from large pools of donor plasma:

- Normal immunoglobulin: contains antibodies to viruses that are common in the population. Intramuscular normal immunoglobulin may be used to protect susceptible contacts against hepatitis A, measles or rubella. High-dose intravenous immunoglobulin is used as replacement therapy in patients with severe immunoglobulin deficiency and in the treatment of autoimmune diseases such as idiopathic thrombocytopenic purpura (ITP).
- Specific immunoglobulins: made from selected donors with high antibody levels to the target of treatment. Examples include tetanus, hepatitis B and rabies immunoglobulins as well as anti-D immunoglobulin for the prevention of maternal sensitisation to RhD in pregnancy (see Chapter 9).

# 4

**SAFE TRANSFUSION – RIGHT BLOOD, RIGHT PATIENT, RIGHT TIME AND RIGHT PLACE**

# Essentials

- Avoid unnecessary and inappropriate transfusions.
- Preventable 'wrong blood into patient' incidents are nearly always caused by human error and may cause fatal reactions due to ABO incompatibility.
- Most mistransfusion incidents are caused by identification errors at the time of pre-transfusion blood sampling, sample handling in the laboratory, collecting the wrong component from the blood bank or transfusion to the patient.
- The identity check between patient and blood component is the crucial final opportunity to avoid potentially fatal mistransfusion.
- At every stage of the blood administration process the key elements are positive patient identification, excellent communication and good documentation. These can be enhanced by the use of electronic transfusion management systems and barcode technology.
- Hospitals should develop local transfusion policies based on national guidelines and ensure all staff involved in the clinical transfusion process are appropriately trained and competency assessed.
- Where possible, patients should give 'valid consent' for transfusion based on appropriate information and discussion, but signed consent is not a legal requirement.
- Non-essential 'out of hours' requests for transfusion and overnight administration of blood should be avoided wherever possible because of an increased risk of errors.

Data from the UK Serious Hazards of Transfusion (SHOT) initiative (http://www.shotuk.org) show that around 1 in 13000 blood units are administered to the wrong patient with occasional fatal outcomes. 'Wrong blood into patient' incidents are preventable and nearly always caused by human error. The root cause of most incidents is misidentification at the time of pre-transfusion blood sampling, laboratory testing, collecting the blood component from the blood bank or administration of the transfusion at the bedside. Potentially fatal ABO-incompatible transfusions still occur although improved clinical policies, staff training and introduction of methods to improve identification, resulting from the various Better Blood Transfusion initiatives, has significantly reduced their number over the last decade. Avoiding unnecessary or inappropriate transfusions is an essential starting point for safe transfusion practice.

The British Committee for Standards in Haematology (BCSH) *Guideline on the Administration of Blood Components* (2009) (http://www.bcshguidelines.com) describes the essentials of safe requesting, collection and administration of blood components (summarised in Table 4.1) and should form the basis of local transfusion policies.

The key principles that underpin every stage of the blood administration process are:

- Positive patient identification
- Good documentation
- Excellent communication.

**Table 4.1 Safe blood administration (adapted from the BCSH *Guideline on Administration of Blood Components*, 2009, with permission)**

| | |
|---|---|
| Positive patient identification | Positive patient identification at all stages of the transfusion process is essential. Minimum patient identifiers are:<br>• Last name, first name, date of birth, unique identification number.<br>• Whenever possible ask patients to state their full name and date of birth. For patients who are unable to identify themselves (paediatric, unconscious, confused or language barrier) seek verification of identity from a parent or carer **at the bedside**. This must exactly match the information on the identity band (or equivalent).<br>• All paperwork relating to the patient must include, and be identical in every detail, to the minimum patient identifiers on the identity band. |
| Patient information and consent for transfusion | Where possible, patients (and for children, those with parental responsibility) should have the risks, benefits and alternatives to transfusion explained to them in a timely and understandable manner. Standardised patient information, such as national patient information leaflets, should be used wherever possible. |
| Pre-transfusion documentation | Minimum dataset in patient's clinical record:<br>• Reason for transfusion (clinical and laboratory data).<br>• Summary of information provided to patient (benefits, risks, alternatives) and patient consent. |
| Prescription (authorisation) | The transfusion 'prescription' must contain the minimum patient identifiers and specify:<br>• Components to be transfused<br>• Date of transfusion<br>• Volume/number of units to be transfused and the rate or duration of transfusion<br>• Special requirements (e.g. irradiated, CMV negative). |
| Requests for transfusion | Must include:<br>• Minimum patient identifiers and gender<br>• Diagnosis, any significant co-morbidities and reason for transfusion<br>• Component required, volume/number of units and special requirements<br>• Time and location of transfusion<br>• Name and contact number of requester. |
| Blood samples for pre-transfusion testing | **All patients being sampled must be positively identified.**<br>• Collection of the blood sample from the patient into the sample tubes and sample labelling must be a continuous, uninterrupted event involving one patient and one trained and competency assessed healthcare worker.<br>• Sample tubes must not be pre-labelled.<br>• The request form should be signed by the person collecting the sample. |

| Collection and delivery of blood component to clinical area | • Before collection, ensure the patient (and staff) is ready to start transfusion and there is good venous access. |
| | • Only trained and competent staff should collect blood from transfusion laboratory or satellite refrigerator. |
| | • Authorised documentation with minimum patient identifiers must be checked against label on blood component. |
| | • Minimum patient identifiers, date and time of collection and staff member ID must be recorded. |
| | • Deliver to clinical area without delay. |
| Administration to patient | • The final check must be conducted next to the patient by a trained and competent healthcare professional **who also administers the component**. |
| | • All patients being transfused must be positively identified. |
| | • Minimum patient identifiers on the patient's identity band must exactly match those on blood component label. |
| | • All components must be given through a blood administration set (170–200 µm integral mesh filter). |
| | • Transfusion should be completed within 4 hours of leaving controlled temperature storage. |
| Monitoring the patient | Patients should be under regular visual observation and, for every unit transfused, **minimum** monitoring should include: |
| | • Pre-transfusion pulse (P), blood pressure (BP), temperature (T) and respiratory rate (RR). |
| | • P, BP and T 15 minutes after start of transfusion – if significant change, check RR as well. |
| | • If there are any symptoms or signs of a possible reaction – monitor and record P, BP, T and RR and take appropriate action. |
| | • Post-transfusion P, BP and T – not more than 60 minutes after transfusion completed. |
| | • Inpatients observed over next 24 hours and outpatients advised to report late symptoms (24-hour access to clinical advice). |
| Completion of transfusion episode | • If further units are prescribed, **repeat the administration/identity check with each unit**. |
| | • If no further units are prescribed, remove the blood administration set and ensure all transfusion documentation is completed. |

# 4.1 Patient identification

A patient identification band (or risk-assessed equivalent) should be worn by all patients receiving a blood transfusion. The minimum identifiers on the band are:

■ Last name
■ First name
■ Date of birth

*4 Safe transfusion - right blood, right patient, right time and right place*

31

■ Unique patient ID number (wherever possible a national number such as the NHS No. in England and Wales, CHI No. in Scotland or HSC No. in Northern Ireland).

In emergency situations or where the patient cannot be immediately identified at least one unique identifier, such as A&E or trauma number, and patient gender should be used.

Wherever possible, patients for blood sampling or transfusion should be asked to state their full name and date of birth and this must exactly match the information on the identification band. To ensure accuracy and legibility, the ID band should be printed from the hospital's computerised patient administration system, ideally at the bedside. Otherwise, verification of identity should be obtained, if possible, from a parent or carer at the bedside and checked against the identification band. **Identification discrepancies at any stage of the transfusion process must be investigated and resolved before moving to the next stage.**

Identification of patients, samples and blood components throughout the transfusion process can be enhanced by the use of electronic transfusion management systems using barcodes on ID bands and blood components and hand-held scanners linked to the laboratory information systems. Most UK hospitals still use manual ID checks at the bedside although electronic 'blood-tracking' systems to control access to blood refrigerators are in more widespread use.

# 4.2   Documentation

The documentation required at each stage of the transfusion process should be kept to an essential minimum and, whether hard copy or electronic, be 'user-friendly' to encourage compliance by busy clinical teams. Combined transfusion prescription and monitoring charts or care pathways can be used to record the information and provide a clear audit trail. The development of standardised transfusion documentation in the UK has the potential to reduce errors by clinical staff moving between hospitals. All transfusion documentation should include the minimum patient identifiers. Documentation in the clinical record should include:

**Pre-transfusion:**
■ The reason for transfusion, including relevant clinical and laboratory data.
■ The risks, benefits and alternatives to transfusion that have been discussed with the patient and documentation of consent (see below).
■ The components to be transfused and their dose/volume and rate.
■ Any special requirements, such as irradiated components.

**During transfusion:**
■ Details of staff members starting the transfusion.
■ Date and time transfusion started and completed.
■ Donation number of the blood component.
■ Record of observations made before, during and after transfusion.

**Post-transfusion:**
■ Management and outcome of any transfusion reactions or other adverse events.
■ Whether the transfusion achieved the desired outcome (e.g. improvement in symptoms, Hb increment).

## 4.3    Communication

Verbal communication between clinical staff and the laboratory risks misunderstanding or transcription error. Written or electronic communication should be used wherever possible although requests for urgent transfusion should be supplemented by telephone discussion with laboratory staff. Good communication is especially important at times of staff handover between shifts, both on the wards and in the laboratory, and can be enhanced by a standardised and documented process.

## 4.4    Patient consent

The Advisory Committee on the Safety of Blood, Tissues and Organs (SaBTO) recommends that 'valid consent' for blood transfusion should be obtained and documented in the clinical record (signed consent for transfusion is not mandatory, but may be a local requirement). This is underpinned by the following recommendations:

- Use of standardised sources of information for all patients in the UK – appropriate information leaflets are available from the UK Transfusion Services and should be used in all hospitals.
- Use of a standardised information resource for clinicians, indicating the key areas to be discussed when obtaining consent – an example is available from http://www.transfusionguidelines.org.uk/index.asp?Publication=BBT&Section=22&pageid=7691.
- As with any emergency treatment, the need for consent must not prevent or delay essential urgent transfusion, but the presence of a valid Advance Decision Document declining transfusion should always be respected (see Chapter 12). Patients transfused when it is not possible to obtain prior consent should be provided with information retrospectively. This is important, as transfused patients are no longer eligible to act as blood donors. For the same reason, patients who have given consent for possible transfusion during surgery should be informed if they actually received blood while under anaesthesia.
- Patients needing long-term transfusion support should have a modified form of consent (e.g. annual review and re-consent) and this should be specified in local policies.

## 4.5    Authorising (or 'prescribing') the transfusion

Blood components are not licensed medicines and their 'prescription' is not legally restricted to registered medical practitioners. There are clear advantages in terms of safety and efficiency in allowing non-medical practitioners, especially those working in specialist areas such as clinical haematology or oncology, to authorise transfusion in defined situations. A framework has been developed in the UK to allow 'appropriately trained, competent practitioners' such as registered nurses and midwives to make the clinical decision and provide the written instruction for blood component transfusion and this is available on http://www.transfusionguidelines.org.uk/docs/pdfs/BTFramework-final010909.pdf.

All transfusion 'prescriptions' (written authorisation to transfuse) must contain the patient's minimum identifiers and specify the component, dose/volume, rate of transfusion and any special requirements. It should remain a permanent part of the clinical record.

4 Safe transfusion – right blood, right patient, right time and right place

# 4.6 Requests for transfusion

Hospital policies should define which clinical staff are authorised to request blood and what training they need. Telephoned requests for blood components should be kept to an essential minimum because of the risk of transcription errors. Non-urgent 'out of hours' requests should be avoided wherever possible as SHOT data clearly show an increased risk of errors. Computerised physician order entry (CPOE) systems can reduce errors and provide useful guidance to the requesting clinician. Transfusion requests (whether written or electronic) should contain the following information:

- Minimum patient identifiers plus gender (which may be essential for component selection) – BCSH guidelines recommend that organisations have a 'zero tolerance' policy for amending or adding to the 'core identifiers' once a request is submitted.
- Diagnosis and any other clinically relevant information plus the reason for transfusion (not just 'pre-op' or 'anaemia') as this helps laboratory staff select appropriate components and facilitates audit. This may also be helped by the use of standardised indication codes for transfusion, such as those developed by the English National Blood Transfusion Committee (http://www.transfusionguidelines.org.uk/docs/pdfs/nbtc_2014_04_recs_indication_codes_2013.pdf).
- Time, location and urgency of transfusion.
- Relevant information on previous reactions, blood group antibodies or pregnancies.
- Type and dose or volume of blood component required.
- Any special requirements (e.g. irradiated, CMV negative).

# 4.7 Pre-transfusion blood sampling

Misidentification at blood sampling may lead to fatal ABO-incompatible blood transfusion, especially if the patient has not previously had their blood group documented. Inadequately or mislabelled samples carry a significantly increased risk of containing blood from the wrong patient. Risk of misidentification may be reduced by electronic systems, but all sampling should be carried out in line with the following principles by trained and competent staff:

- Patients must be positively identified and their details must match those on the request form.
- All inpatients must wear an identity band (or risk-assessed equivalent).
- Collection of the sample and labelling of the sample tubes must be performed as one uninterrupted process involving one member of staff and one patient.
- **Sample tubes must never be pre-labelled.**
- The sample tube label must contain the minimum patient identifiers (exactly matching those on the request form and identity band), date and time of sampling and identity of person taking the sample.
- Labels printed away from the patient (e.g. addressograph labels) must not be used on the transfusion sample but labels printed 'on demand' and applied to the tube next to the patient, as used in some electronic ID systems, are acceptable.
- All handwritten labels must be legible.
- BCSH guidelines recommend that laboratories have a 'zero tolerance' policy for rejecting samples that do not meet the above minimum requirements.

## 4.8 Collection of blood components and delivery to clinical areas

Errors in collection are a frequent root cause of wrong blood into patient events. All staff responsible for collecting blood from the transfusion laboratory or satellite refrigerators must be trained and competency assessed according to local policies. Manual documentation of collection, such as a 'transfusion register', has been traditionally used but the process can be strengthened by the use of electronic 'blood-tracking' systems.

■ Staff collecting blood must carry documentation, such as a blood collection slip or the transfusion prescription, which contains the minimum patient identifiers. This must be checked against the details on the laboratory-generated label attached to the blood component pack.
■ Computerised blood-tracking systems using barcodes can check (and record) the identity and accreditation of the person collecting or returning the blood (e.g. by scanning a barcode on their ID badge), ensure that the details on the collection documents match those on the selected blood pack and that the blood is within its expiry time and date. Computer-controlled satellite blood refrigerators are also now available that will only allow access to blood components compatible with the appropriate patient. These are ideal for 'remote issue' of blood components at locations without an on-site transfusion laboratory.
■ The Blood Safety and Quality Regulations (BSQR) require that the time a component is out of a controlled temperature environment is recorded and 'cold chain' data must be kept for 15 years. Red cells that have been out of controlled refrigeration for more than 30 minutes must not be reissued for transfusion. (The rationale for the '30-minute rule' is often questioned as it is based on studies carried out many years ago on very different blood components. Recent research shows that red cells show no impairment of function up to 60 minutes out of controlled refrigeration but evidence of bacterial safety is needed before a change in policy can be recommended.)
■ Emergency group O stock in the blood refrigerator must be clearly identified and separated from units labelled for specific patients. The laboratory must be informed immediately when emergency stock is removed so that it can be replenished and an audit trail maintained.

## 4.9 Receiving blood in the clinical area

Before collecting blood components from the blood bank, the clinical staff should ensure the patient is wearing an identity band and has given consent for transfusion, the transfusion 'prescription' has been completed correctly, there is patent venous access and staff are available to start the transfusion promptly and monitor it properly. Only one unit should be collected at a time unless rapid transfusion of large quantities is required (e.g. major haemorrhage). The arrival of components in the clinical area should be documented and the transfusion started as soon as possible.

# 4.10  Administration to the patient

The identity check between patient and blood component (Figure 4.1) is the final opportunity to avoid potentially fatal mistransfusion ('the last chance saloon'). The check must be performed for every unit transfused. The key principles of safe bedside administration are:

- Blood components must be administered by registered practitioners who are trained and competent according to local policies.
- The final check must take place next to the patient, **not at the nursing station or another remote area.**
- There is no evidence that either one or two staff performing the bedside check is safer and local policy should be followed. If two people perform the check, each should perform it independently.
- If the checking process is interrupted, it must start again.
- Transfusion must only go ahead if the details on the patient identity band (positively confirmed by the patient if possible), the laboratory-generated label attached to the component pack and the transfusion prescription are an exact match. Any discrepancy must immediately be reported to the transfusion laboratory.
- Check the expiry date of the component and ensure the donation number and blood group on the pack matches that on the laboratory-generated label attached to the pack.
- Any special requirements on the transfusion prescription, such as irradiated component, must be checked against the label on the pack.
- Inspect the component pack for signs of leakage, discoloration or clumps.
- A 'compatibility report form' issued by the laboratory and the patient's clinical records **must not** form part of the bedside identity check ('checking paper against paper'). Compatibility report forms are generated by the same laboratory computer used to produce the laboratory-generated label on the blood pack and the two will always match (even if the blood is being presented to the wrong patient). It is strongly recommended (BCSH and National Patient Safety Agency (www.npsa.nhs.uk)) that laboratories do not issue compatibility report forms to avoid their inappropriate use in the final administration check.
- The prescription and other associated paperwork should be signed by the person administering the component and the component donation number, date, time of starting and stopping the transfusion, dose/volume of component transfused and name of the administering practitioner should be recorded in the clinical record.
- To reduce the risk of bacterial transmission, blood component transfusions should be completed within 4 hours of removal from a controlled temperature environment.
- Non-essential overnight transfusion of blood should be avoided, except in adequately staffed specialist clinical areas, because of the increased risk of errors.

# 4.11  Monitoring the transfusion episode

Transfusion observations should be recorded on a dedicated transfusion record or electronic device that can generate a report for filing in the clinical record. Minimum monitoring of each unit transfused should include:

- Regular visual observation of the patient during the transfusion and encouragement to report new symptoms.
- Baseline pulse rate, blood pressure (BP), temperature and respiratory rate (RR) must be recorded no more than 60 minutes pre-transfusion.

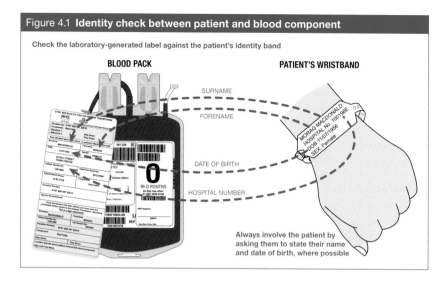

**Figure 4.1 Identity check between patient and blood component**

Check the laboratory-generated label against the patient's identity band

BLOOD PACK

PATIENT'S WRISTBAND

SURNAME

FORENAME

DATE OF BIRTH

HOSPITAL NUMBER

Always involve the patient by asking them to state their name and date of birth, where possible

- Pulse, BP and temperature should be checked around 15 minutes after the start of transfusion (many serious reactions, such as ABO incompatibility or bacterial transmission present early in the transfusion episode). If any of these observations have changed, check RR as well.
- If the patient reports new symptoms, repeat the baseline observations and take appropriate action (see Chapter 5).
- Check pulse, BP and temperature not more than 60 minutes after the end of the transfusion (and as a baseline before any further units are transfused).
- Inpatients should be observed for late reactions over the next 24 hours and day-care patients advised to report symptoms developing after discharge (preferably with issue of a 'Contact Card' giving access to immediate clinical advice).

# 4.12  Technical aspects of transfusion

## 4.12.1  Intravenous access

Blood components can be transfused through most peripheral or central venous catheters, although the flow rate is reduced by narrow lumen catheters and long peripherally inserted central catheters (PICC lines).

They should be transfused through an administration set with a 170–200 μm integral mesh filter. Paediatric administration sets with a smaller prime volume are available for small-volume transfusions. Although special platelet administration sets are available, it is safe to use a standard blood administration set, but platelets should not be transfused through a set previously used for red cells as some platelet loss will occur. It is not necessary to prime or flush blood administration sets with physiological (0.9%) saline but a new administration set should be used if blood components are followed by another infusion fluid. Although there is little evidence, current guidelines recommend changing blood administration sets at least every 12 hours to reduce the risk of bacterial infection.

Blood and other solutions can be infused through the separate lumens of multi-lumen central venous catheters as rapid dilution occurs in the bloodstream. Where possible, one lumen should be reserved for the administration of blood components.

## 4.12.2 Infusion devices

There are two main types: gravity delivered or infusion pumps. Devices must be CE marked and used according to the manufacturer's instructions (including the use of compatible administration sets). Infusion devices must be maintained in accordance with the manufacturer's guidelines and the pre-administration check should include a check of the device and its settings. The device should be monitored regularly during transfusion to ensure the correct volume is being delivered at the correct rate.

## 4.12.3 Rapid infusion devices

These are used in situations such as major haemorrhage. Infusion rates range from 6 to 30 L/hour and most incorporate a blood-warming device. They should be used with a large-gauge venous access catheter.

## 4.12.4 Blood warmers

Rapid infusion of red cells recently removed from the refrigerator may cause hypothermia. Concerns include impaired coagulation in surgical or trauma patients and cardiac arrhythmias if cold blood is transfused rapidly into a central catheter or in neonates and small infants having large-volume transfusions. The National Institute for Health and Care Excellence (NICE) in England recommends that, in all patients undergoing elective or emergency surgery, 'intravenous fluids (500 mL or more) and blood products should be warmed to 37°C'.

Blood warmers may also be used in patients with clinically significant cold antibodies (discuss with a transfusion medicine specialist).

Only CE-marked blood warmers should be used. Some operate up to 43°C but are safe if used in accordance with the manufacturer's instructions. Improvised blood-warming, such as immersion of the pack in hot water, in a microwave or on a radiator must never be used.

## 4.12.5 Compatible intravenous fluids

It is good practice to avoid the co-administration of any intravenous fluid through the same line used for blood components, unless a multi-lumen central venous catheter is used. Solutions containing calcium (e.g. Ringer's lactate) or calcium-containing colloids (e.g. Haemaccel™ or Gelofusine™) antagonise citrate anticoagulant and may allow clots to form if mixed in the same infusion line. Hypotonic solutions, such as 5% dextrose in water, can cause haemolysis of red cells in laboratory experiments but the clinical significance of this is uncertain and no clinical adverse events have been reported.

## 4.12.6 Co-administration of intravenous drugs and blood

Drugs should never be added to a blood component bag.

Wherever possible, intravenous drugs should be administered between transfusions or administered through a second venous access device (or the separate lumen of a multi-lumen central venous catheter). If this is not possible, the transfusion should be temporarily stopped and the line flushed with 0.9% saline before and after administration of the drug.

Some patients using patient-controlled analgesia (PCA) devices delivering opioid pain killers, such as those on palliative care or with sickle cell pain crises, have very poor peripheral venous access and it is convenient (and kind) to use the administration line used for transfusion. Standard concentrations of morphine, hydromorphone or meperidine have no harmful effect on co-administered red cells.

## 4.13  Transfusion of blood components

Table 4.2 summarises key points about the transfusion of commonly used components in adult patients (see Chapter 10 for administration of components in paediatric/neonatal practice). Clinical use of blood components is discussed in Chapters 7–10.

**Table 4.2** Blood component administration to adults (doses and transfusion rates are for guidance only and depend on clinical indication) (based on BCSH *Guideline on the Administration of Blood Components*, 2009, with permission)

| Blood component | Notes on administration |
|---|---|
| Red cells in additive solution | Transfusions must be completed within 4 hours of removal from controlled temperature storage. |
| | Many patients can be safely transfused over 90–120 minutes per unit. |
| | A dose of 4 mL/kg raises Hb concentration by approximately 10 g/L. Note: The common belief that one red cell pack = 10 g/L increment only applies to patients around 70 kg weight – the risk of transfusion-associated circulatory overload (TACO) is reduced by careful pre-transfusion clinical assessment and use of single-unit transfusions, or prescription in millilitres, for elderly or small, frail adults where appropriate. |
| | During major haemorrhage, very rapid transfusion (each unit over 5–10 minutes) may be required. |
| Platelets | One adult therapeutic dose (ATD) (pool of four units derived from whole blood donations or single-donor apheresis unit) typically raises the platelet count by $20–40 \times 10^9$/L. |
| | Usually transfused over 30–60 minutes per ATD. |
| | Platelets should not be transfused through a giving-set already used for other blood components. |
| | Start transfusion as soon as possible after component arrives in the clinical area. |
| Fresh frozen plasma (FFP) | Dose typically 12–15 mL/kg, determined by clinical indication, pre-transfusion and post-transfusion coagulation tests and clinical response. |
| | Infusion rate typically 10–20 mL/kg/hour, although more rapid transfusion may be appropriate when treating coagulopathy in major haemorrhage. |
| | Because of the high volumes required to produce a haemostatic benefit, patients receiving FFP must have careful haemodynamic monitoring to prevent TACO. |
| | FFP should not be used to reverse warfarin (prothrombin complex is a specific and effective antidote). |
| Cryoprecipitate | Typical adult dose is two five-donor pools (ten single-donor units). |
| | Will raise fibrinogen concentration by approximately 1 g/L in average adult. |
| | Typically administered at 10–20 mL/kg/hour (30–60 min per five-unit pool). |

# 5

**ADVERSE EFFECTS
OF TRANSFUSION**

# Essentials

- Modern blood transfusion is very safe but preventable death and major morbidity still occurs.
- Inappropriate decisions to transfuse put patients at unnecessary risk of transfusion errors, reactions and transfusion-transmitted infection.
- Identification errors (of patients, blood samples and blood components) by hospital staff are the root cause of most 'wrong blood into patient' incidents, including ABO-incompatible transfusions.
- Severe acute transfusion reactions are the most common cause of major morbidity. These include immunological reactions (predominantly allergy/anaphylaxis, haemolytic reactions and lung injury), circulatory overload and rare bacterial contamination of blood components.
- If a serious transfusion reaction is suspected – **stop the transfusion**; assess clinically and start resuscitation if necessary; **check** that the details on the patient's ID band and the compatibility label of the blood component match; **call** for medical assistance; **contact** the transfusion laboratory.
- Transfusion-transmitted infection is now a very rare event, underpinned by voluntary donation, donor selection procedures and microbiological testing, but constant vigilance is required as new threats emerge.
- Variant CJD transmission by blood has had a major impact on transfusion practice in the UK although the risk appears to be receding.

Compared with many medical and surgical procedures modern blood transfusion is extremely safe but deaths and major morbidity still do occur. Errors in the identification of patients, blood samples and blood components are the root cause of many preventable serious adverse events (see Chapter 4). Around 1 in 13000 blood component units is transfused to the wrong patient (not always with adverse consequences) and up to 1 in 1300 pre-transfusion blood samples are taken from the wrong patient.

Serious acute transfusion reactions are often unpredictable but patients are put at unnecessary risk by inappropriate decisions to transfuse. In its 2012 Annual Report, the UK Serious Hazards of Transfusion haemovigilance scheme (SHOT – http://www.shotuk.org/) described 252 incidents of 'incorrect blood component transfused' (each underpinned by 100 near misses). Ten ABO-incompatible transfusions (all due to clinical errors) and 145 incidents of 'avoidable, delayed or under-transfusion' were reported. There were nine transfusion-related deaths (six associated with transfusion-associated circulatory overload) and 134 cases of major morbidity (most often following acute transfusion reactions).

Transfusion-transmitted infection is now a rare event but there is no room for complacency as the emergence of new infectious agents requires constant vigilance.

## 5.1  Haemovigilance

Haemovigilance is the 'systematic surveillance of adverse reactions and adverse events related to transfusion' with the aim of improving transfusion safety. Transfusion reactions and adverse events should be investigated by the clinical team and hospital transfusion team and reviewed by the hospital transfusion committee. SHOT invites voluntary reporting of serious adverse transfusion reactions, errors and events as well as near-miss incidents. Under the Blood Safety and Quality Regulations 2005 (BSQR) there is a legal requirement to report serious adverse reactions and events to the Medicines and Healthcare Products Regulatory Agency (MHRA). The MHRA also inspects blood establishments (transfusion centres) and hospital transfusion laboratories to ensure their processes and quality standards comply with the BSQR. SHOT and MHRA work closely together and have a joint reporting system through the SABRE IT system (http://www.mhra.gov.uk/ Safetyinformation/Reportingsafetyproblems/Blood/).

Haemovigilance can identify transfusion hazards and demonstrate the effectiveness of interventions. SHOT reporting highlighted the importance of transfusion-related acute lung injury (TRALI) as a potentially lethal risk of transfusion and confirmed the benefit of sourcing fresh frozen plasma (FFP) from male donors. More recently, transfusion-associated circulatory overload (TACO) has been identified as an important preventable cause of death or major morbidity. Incidents of avoidable, delayed or under-transfusion are increasingly reported, leading to initiatives to improve the knowledge base of clinical staff and awareness of evidence-based guidelines.

Adverse effects of transfusion are commonly classified as infectious or non-infectious; acute or delayed; caused by errors or pathological reactions; and by their severity (mild, moderate or severe).

## 5.2 Non-infectious hazards of transfusion

### 5.2.1 Acute transfusion reactions

Acute transfusion reactions (ATRs) present within 24 hours of transfusion and vary in severity from mild febrile or allergic reactions to life-threatening events. They include:

- Febrile non-haemolytic transfusion reactions – usually clinically mild.
- Allergic transfusion reactions – ranging from mild urticaria to life-threatening angio-oedema or anaphylaxis.
- Acute haemolytic transfusion reactions – e.g. ABO incompatibility.
- Bacterial contamination of blood unit – range from mild pyrexial reactions to rapidly lethal septic shock depending on species.
- Transfusion-associated circulatory overload (TACO).
- Transfusion-related acute lung injury (TRALI).

Early recognition of ATRs by careful monitoring of vital signs during transfusion is important; especially the 15-minute checks (see Chapter 4). Patients should be asked to report symptoms that arise during the transfusion and for at least the next 24 hours.

Severe ATRs occur in about 1 in 7000 units transfused. Patients may present suddenly with cardiovascular collapse and the underlying cause may not be immediately apparent. The differential diagnosis of severe, life-threatening ATRs includes bacterial transfusion-transmitted infection, acute haemolytic reactions (usually due to ABO-incompatible transfusion), anaphylaxis, TRALI and TACO.

The British Committee for Standards in Haematology (BCSH) *Guideline on the Investigation and Management of Acute Transfusion Reactions* (Tinegate et al., 2012) (http://www. bcshguidelines.com) emphasises that immediate management should focus on timely recognition of the event and its severity, based on clinical symptoms and signs, stopping the transfusion and resuscitating the patient. This is followed by appropriate investigation, specific treatment and prevention (where possible) of future events. The guideline provides a flowchart for the recognition and management of ATR based on presenting symptoms and clinical signs (Figure 5.1).

Key principles in the management of ATR include:

- Transfusing patients in clinical areas where they can be directly observed by appropriately trained staff (including the emergency management of anaphylaxis)
- Ensuring that the recognition and immediate management of ATR are incorporated into local transfusion policies and the training of clinical and laboratory staff.

If a patient develops new symptoms or signs during a transfusion:

- Stop the transfusion and maintain venous access with physiological saline.
- Check vital signs and start resuscitation if necessary.
- As soon as possible, check that the identification details of the patient, their ID band and the compatibility label of the component match.
- Inspect the component for abnormal clumps or discoloration.
- If the presumed ATR is severe or life threatening the transfusion must be discontinued and immediate medical review arranged.
- Note: If a patient being transfused for haemorrhage develops hypotension, careful clinical assessment is essential as this may be due to continuing blood loss and continuation of the transfusion may be life-saving.

Except for patients with mild allergic or febrile reactions, a standard battery of tests should be performed, including full blood count, renal and liver function tests and assessment of urine for Hb. Further tests are determined by the symptoms and clinical signs (Table 5.1).

## 5.2.2 Severe and life-threatening reactions

### 5.2.2.1 Acute haemolytic reactions

The most serious reactions are caused by transfusion of ABO-incompatible red cells which react with the patient's anti-A or anti-B antibodies. There is rapid destruction of the transfused red cells in the circulation (intravascular haemolysis) and the release of inflammatory cytokines. The patient often quickly becomes shocked and may develop acute renal failure and disseminated intravascular coagulation (DIC). Transfusion of less than 30 mL of group A red cells to a group O patient has proven fatal. Acute haemolysis may also, rarely, be caused by transfusing plasma-rich blood components, such as platelets or FFP (usually group O) containing high-titre or high-potency anti-A or anti-B antibodies to a patient with group A, B or AB red cells. This has mainly been reported in infants and small children (see Chapter 10). Intravenous immunoglobulin solutions contain ABO antibodies and the 2012 annual report for SHOT includes a rare case of fatality due to haemolysis and renal failure in a group A patient.

ABO-incompatible transfusion occurs in around 1 in 180 000 red cell units transfused. It is usually caused by human error when taking or labelling pre-transfusion blood samples, collecting components from the blood bank or satellite refrigerator and/or failing to perform a correct identity check of blood pack and patient at the bedside (see Chapter 4). If red cells are transfused to the wrong patient, there is around a 30% chance they will be ABO incompatible. Major morbidity (requiring intensive care or renal dialysis) occurs in up to 30% of cases and 5–10% of episodes contribute to the death of the patient.

Figure 5.1 **Clinical flowchart for the management of acute transfusion reactions (reproduced from BCSH** *Guideline on the Investigation and Management of Acute Transfusion Reactions,* **2012, with kind permission of British Committee for Standards in Haematology)**

**PATIENT EXHIBITING POSSIBLE FEATURES OF AN ACUTE TRANSFUSION REACTION, WHICH MAY INCLUDE:**

fever, chills, rigors, tachycardia, hyper- or hypotension, collapse, flushing, urticaria, pain (bone, muscle, chest, abdominal), respiratory distress, nausea, general malaise

**STOP THE TRANSFUSION:** undertake rapid clinical assessment, check patient ID/blood compatibility level, visually assess unit

Evidence of:

Life-threatening Airway and/or Breathing and/or Circulatory problems and/or wrong blood given and/or evidence of contaminated unit

**Yes**

**No**

**Inform medical staff**

**SEVERE/LIFE-THREATENING**

- Call for urgent medical help
- Initiate resuscitation ABC
- Is haemorrhage likely to be causing hypotension? If not, discontinue transfusion (do not discard implicated unit/s)
- Maintain venous access
- Monitor patient, e.g. TPR, BP, urinary output, oxygen saturations

**MODERATE**

- Temperature ≥ 39°C or rise ≥ 2°C and/or
- Other symptoms/signs apart from pruritus/rash only

- Consider bacterial contamination if the temperature rises as above and review patient's underlying condition and transfusion history
- Monitor patient more frequently e.g. TPR, BP, oxygen saturations, urinary output

**MILD**

- Isolated temperature ≥ 38°C and rise of 1–2°C and/or
- Pruritus/rash only

- Continue transfusion
- Consider symptomatic treatment
- Monitor patient more frequently as for moderate reactions
- If symptoms/signs worsen, manage as moderate/severe reaction (see left)

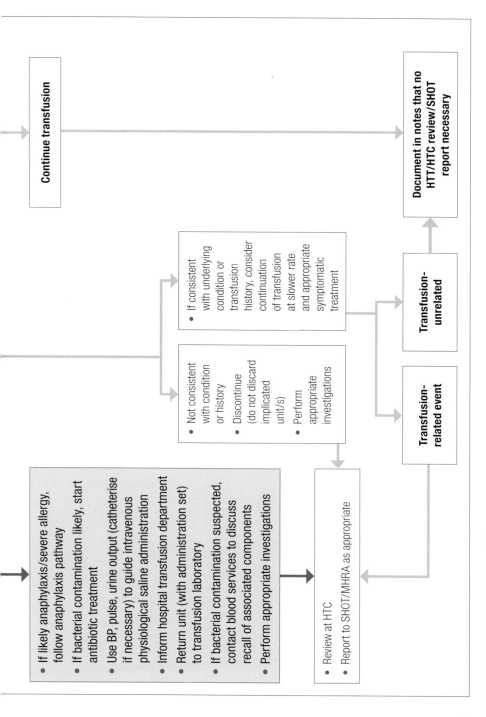

Continue transfusion

- If likely anaphylaxis/severe allergy, follow anaphylaxis pathway
- If bacterial contamination likely, start antibiotic treatment
- Use BP, pulse, urine output (catheterise if necessary) to guide intravenous physiological saline administration
- Inform hospital transfusion department
- Return unit (with administration set) to transfusion laboratory
- If bacterial contamination suspected, contact blood services to discuss recall of associated components
- Perform appropriate investigations

- Review at HTC
- Report to SHOT/MHRA as appropriate

Not consistent with condition or history
- Discontinue (do not discard implicated unit/s)
- Perform appropriate investigations

If consistent with underlying condition or transfusion history, consider continuation of transfusion at slower rate and appropriate symptomatic treatment

Transfusion-related event

Transfusion-unrelated

Document in notes that no HTT/HTC review/SHOT report necessary

5 Adverse effects of transfusion

**Table 5.1 Investigation of moderate or severe acute transfusion reactions (adapted from BCSH *Guideline on the Investigation and Management of Acute Transfusion Reactions*, 2012)**

| Symptoms | Investigations |
|---|---|
| Fever (>2°C rise or >39°C) and/or chills, rigors, myalgia, nausea or vomiting and/or loin pain | Standard investigations[a] |
| | Samples for repeat compatibility testing, direct antiglobulin test (DAT ), lactate dehydrogenase (LDH) and haptoglobins |
| | Blood cultures from patient |
| | Coagulation screen |
| | **Do not discard implicated unit** |
| | If febrile reaction sustained, return blood component to laboratory, repeat serological investigations (compatibility testing, antibody screen and DAT), measure haptoglobins and culture blood component. **Contact a Blood Service consultant to discuss the need for recall of components from same donation**. |
| Mucosal swelling (angioedema) | Standard investigations[a] |
| | Measure IgA level – if <0.07 g/L (in absence of generalised hypogammaglobulinaemia) perform confirmatory test with sensitive method and check for IgA antibodies |
| Dyspnoea, wheeze or features of anaphylaxis | Standard investigations[a] |
| | Check $O_2$ saturation or blood gases |
| | Chest X-ray (mandatory if symptoms severe) |
| | If severe or moderate allergic reaction suspected, measure IgA level (as above) |
| | If severe allergic/anaphylactic reaction, consider measurement of serial mast cell tryptase (immediate, 3 and 24 hours) |
| Hypotension (isolated fall in systolic blood pressure of >30 mm Hg resulting in a level <80 mm Hg) | Standard investigations[a] plus investigations as for fever |
| | If allergic reaction suspected measure IgA level |
| | If severe allergic/anaphylactic reaction suspected, consider measurement of serial mast cell tryptase |

[a] Standard investigations: full blood count, renal and liver function tests, assessment of urine for Hb

Conscious patients often become very unwell within the first few minutes of transfusion, complaining of flushing, loin and abdominal pain and 'a feeling of impending doom'. If the patient is unconscious, anaesthetised or cannot communicate, the first indication of a reaction may be tachycardia, hypotension and bleeding into the skin or from needle wounds, emphasising the importance of careful monitoring of vital signs.

Immediate clinical management of patients with suspected severe acute haemolytic transfusion should follow the steps outlined in Figure 5.1 and the investigations in Table 5.1. After disconnecting the transfusion pack and starting resuscitation:

- Maintain venous access with physiological saline and call for urgent medical support.
- Check the compatibility label on the blood pack against the patient's ID band (and seek confirmation of identity from the patient, parent or carer if possible).
- Inform the transfusion laboratory urgently. If the wrong blood has been transfused, another patient may be at risk. Return the (sealed) transfusion pack and giving-set for investigation.
- Seek early support and advice from critical care and haematology teams and admit the patient to an intensive care unit if possible.

## 5.2.2.2 Transfusion of a blood component contaminated by bacteria

Although rare, this more often occurs with platelet components (which are stored at 22–24°C) than with red cells refrigerated at 2–6°C and can rapidly be fatal. Measures to reduce bacterial contamination from the donor arm have significantly reduced this risk (see section 5.3) but awareness and rapid response are important. The transfusion of a pack contaminated with highly pathogenic bacteria often causes an acute severe reaction soon after the transfusion is started. Initially, this may be indistinguishable from an acute haemolytic reaction or severe allergic reaction. Typical symptoms and signs include rigors, fever (usually >2°C above baseline), hypotension and rapidly developing shock and impaired consciousness.

Immediate management and investigation follows the principles outlined in Figure 5.1 and Table 5.1. In particular:

- Inspection of the pack may show abnormal discoloration, aggregates or offensive smell, but many packs appear normal.
- Blood cultures should be taken from the patient and treatment immediately started with an intravenous broad spectrum antibiotic combination covering gram negative and gram positive bacteria (the local empirical antibiotic regimen used in patients with neutropenic sepsis is appropriate).
- Implicated components must be sealed to avoid leakage or contamination and returned to the transfusion laboratory for further investigation.
- The blood transfusion centre must be contacted immediately so that any associated components from the implicated donation can be urgently identified and withdrawn from hospital blood banks.

National Blood Services provide comprehensive bacterial testing and typing of strains (to confirm identity of contaminating bacteria with those isolated from the patient's blood cultures). Both SHOT and BCSH recommend that, wherever possible, implicated component packs are returned to the Blood Service for testing rather than sampled and cultured in local hospital laboratories.

## 5.2.2.3 Severe allergic or anaphylactic reactions

Shock or severe hypotension associated with wheeze (bronchospasm), stridor from laryngeal oedema or swelling of face, limbs or mucous membranes (angioedema) is strongly suggestive of anaphylaxis – an acute, life-threatening emergency. Other skin changes may include flushing and urticaria ('nettle rash' or hives) that also occur in less severe allergic reactions. Severe allergic and anaphylactic reactions may occur with all blood components but are most commonly reported with plasma-rich components such as platelets or FFP. In addition to the general resuscitation and supportive measures in Figure 5.1, specific points include:

- Staff in clinical areas carrying out blood transfusion must be trained in the emergency management of anaphylaxis, and epinephrine (adrenaline) must be available for emergency use.
- UK Resuscitation Council (UKRC) guidelines (2010 update) (http://www.resus.org.uk/pages/guide.htm) recommend the urgent administration of intramuscular (IM) epinephrine to treat anaphylaxis (adult dose 0.5 mL of 1:1000 (500 µg)). The IM route is rapidly effective (and life-saving) and prevents delay in attempting to obtain venous access in a shocked patient. It is not contraindicated in patients with coagulopathy or low platelet count. The 2012 BCSH guideline on the investigation and management of acute transfusion reactions recommends that intravenous epinephrine is only given by expert practitioners such as anaesthetists.
- Urgent expert medical care should be called immediately (e.g. critical care outreach team or local equivalent).
- After initial resuscitation, parenteral steroids or antihistamines may be given but these should not be the first-line therapy.

After an anaphylactic reaction to blood, further investigation of the patient should be discussed with a clinical immunologist (including diagnosis of severe IgA deficiency – see below). Future transfusion policy should be discussed with a specialist in transfusion medicine. Most patients will have a single anaphylactic episode and essential transfusions should not be withheld (but must be carefully monitored). Those with recurrent episodes may benefit from using washed red cells or platelets in additive solution. There is little evidence to support the common practice of giving prophylactic antihistamines or steroids. Patients with recurrent reactions to FFP may be switched to pooled solvent detergent FFP, which rarely causes severe allergic reactions.

## 5.2.2.4 Severe allergic reactions associated with IgA deficiency

Only a small minority of patients with IgA deficiency are at risk of developing severe allergic reactions to blood components. Those at most risk have severe IgA deficiency (<0.07 g/L), often with anti-IgA antibodies in their plasma. Even then, most such patients do not react to blood transfusion. Patients with less severely reduced IgA levels as part of a more generalised (e.g. common variable immunodeficiency or secondary to a lymphoproliferative disorder) antibody deficiency disorder and the frequent mild cases picked up when screening for IgA coeliac antibodies are not at risk. Patients with no history of severe reactions to blood transfusion should be transfused with standard blood components.

The small group of patients with severe IgA deficiency and a clear history of serious allergic reaction to blood components should be discussed with a specialist in transfusion medicine and/or clinical immunologist. In elective situations they should be transfused with blood components from IgA-deficient donors. The UK Blood Services keep a small stock of such components on the shelf and have panels of suitable donors to call upon. If IgA-deficient components are not available within a clinically relevant time-frame (e.g. acute haemorrhage) then washed red cells should be used (washed platelets resuspended in platelet additive solution still have significant amounts of IgA in the plasma). In extreme emergency, transfusion with standard blood components should not be withheld and the patient must be transfused in a clinical area with appropriate facilities and staff to identify and treat severe allergic reactions.

## 5.2.2.5 *Transfusion-related acute lung injury (TRALI)*

Classical TRALI is caused by antibodies in the donor blood reacting with the patient's neutrophils, monocytes or pulmonary endothelium. Inflammatory cells are sequestered in the lungs, causing leakage of plasma into the alveolar spaces (non-cardiogenic pulmonary oedema). Most cases present within 2 hours of transfusion (maximum 6 hours) with severe breathlessness and cough productive of frothy pink sputum. It is often associated with hypotension (due to loss of plasma volume), fever and rigors and transient peripheral blood neutropenia or monocytopenia. Chest X-ray shows bilateral nodular shadowing in the lung fields with normal heart size. TRALI is often confused with acute heart failure due to circulatory overload (see Table 5.2) and treatment with powerful diuretics may increase mortality.

Treatment is supportive, with high-concentration oxygen therapy and ventilatory support if required. Steroid therapy is not effective. Managed appropriately, often with intensive care, there is now a high rate of survival and most patients recover within 1 to 3 days without long-term problems.

**Table 5.2 Comparison of TRALI and TACO (adapted from *BCSH Guideline on the Investigation and Management of Acute Transfusion Reactions*, 2012, by kind permission of British Committee for Standards in Haematology)**

|  | TRALI | TACO |
|---|---|---|
| Patient characteristics | ? More common in haematology and surgical patients | Most common in age >70 but can occur at any age |
| Implicated blood components | Usually plasma or platelets | Any |
| Onset | Up to 6 hours from transfusion (usually within 2 hours) | Within 6 hours of transfusion |
| Oxygen saturation | Reduced | Reduced |
| Blood pressure | Often low | Often high |
| Jugular venous pressure | Normal or low | Elevated |
| Temperature | Often raised | Normal |
| Chest X-ray | Bilateral peri-hilar and nodular shadowing or 'white out', heart size normal | Enlarged heart and characteristics of pulmonary oedema |
| Echocardiogram | Normal | Abnormal |
| Pulmonary artery wedge pressure | Normal | Elevated |
| Blood count | Fall in neutrophils and monocytes followed by neutrophil leucocytosis | No specific changes |
| Fluid challenge | Improves | Worsens |
| Response to diuretics | Worsens | Improves |

Retrospective confirmation of TRALI requires the demonstration of antibodies in the donor's plasma that react with antigens on the patient's white blood cells. Suspected cases should be reported to the Blood Service and discussed with a transfusion medicine specialist who can advise on the need to investigate the implicated blood donors for antibodies to human leucocyte antigens (HLA) or human neutrophil antigens (HNA) with a view to removing them from the donor panel.

SHOT data suggest an approximate incidence of TRALI of 1 in 150 000 units transfused. It is most common after transfusion of plasma-rich blood components such as FFP or platelets and implicated donors are usually females sensitised during previous pregnancy. Since the UK Blood Services switched to using male donors for producing FFP, resuspending pooled platelets in male plasma and screening female apheresis platelet donors for leucocyte antibodies, SHOT has documented a significant fall in both reported cases and mortality from TRALI.

## 5.2.2.6 Transfusion-associated circulatory overload (TACO)

TACO is defined as acute or worsening pulmonary oedema within 6 hours of transfusion. Typical features include acute respiratory distress, tachycardia, raised blood pressure and evidence of positive fluid balance. It has probably been significantly under-reported in the past and may now be the most common cause of transfusion-related death in developed countries.

TACO causes significant morbidity and mortality. In 2012 SHOT received 82 reports of TACO. It contributed to the death of six patients and was responsible for 29 cases of major morbidity. Elderly patients are at particular risk and predisposing medical conditions include heart failure, renal impairment, low albumin concentration and fluid overload. Small patients, such as the frail elderly and children, are at increased risk of receiving inappropriately high-volume and rapid blood transfusions. Most reported cases involve red cell transfusions but high-volume FFP transfusions, sometimes given inappropriately for reversal of warfarin, have been identified as a risk. Poor pre-transfusion clinical assessment and inadequate monitoring during transfusion is a common feature of reported cases.

The treatment of TACO involves stopping the transfusion and administering oxygen and diuretic therapy with careful monitoring and critical care support if required. The risk of TACO is reduced by careful consideration of the need to transfuse, clinical assessment for predisposing factors, prescription of appropriate volume and flow rate, and adequate monitoring during the procedure. The common assumption that one unit of red cells produces a rise in Hb of 10 g/L only applies to patients of 70–80 kg. A dose of 4 mL/kg will produce a rise of about 10 g/L. The use of single-unit transfusions in small, frail adults or prescription in millilitres (as in paediatric practice) has been recommended.

## 5.2.2.7 Hypotensive reactions

Hypotensive reactions are indicated by an isolated fall in systolic blood pressure of 30 mm Hg or more (to <80 mm Hg) during, or within one hour of, transfusion with no evidence of an allergic reaction or haemorrhage. Most are transient but they occasionally progress to shock and organ dysfunction. The cause of most of these reactions is unknown, although they may be more common in patients taking ACE inhibitors. Management involves stopping the transfusion and nursing the patient flat with leg elevation (or in the 'recovery position' if consciousness is impaired). Other causes of severe ATR should be excluded by clinical and laboratory investigation.

Patients with recurrent hypotensive reactions may be given a trial of washed blood components.

## 5.2.3 Less severe acute transfusion reactions

### 5.2.3.1 Febrile non-haemolytic transfusion reactions (FNHTRs)

FNHTR are characterised by fever, sometimes accompanied by shivering, muscle pain and nausea. These are much less common since leucodepleted blood components were introduced. They can occur up to 2 hours after completion of the transfusion and are more common in multi-transfused patients receiving red cells.

Mild FNHTRs (pyrexia >38°C, but <2°C rise from baseline) can often be managed simply by slowing (or temporarily stopping) the transfusion. Giving an anti-pyretic, such as paracetamol, may be helpful. The patient should be monitored closely in case these are the early signs of a more severe ATR.

In the case of moderate FNHTRs (pyrexia >2°C above baseline or >39°C or rigors and/or myalgia), the transfusion should be stopped. If the symptoms worsen, or do not quickly resolve, consider the possibility of a haemolytic or bacterial reaction. In most cases it is prudent to resume transfusion with a different blood unit.

Patients with recurrent FNHTRs can be pre-medicated with oral paracetamol (or a non-steroidal anti-inflammatory drug if rigors or myalgia are a problem) given at least one hour before the reaction is anticipated, although the evidence base for effectiveness is poor. Patients who continue to react should have a trial of washed blood components.

### 5.2.3.2 Mild allergic reactions

Symptoms are confined to itching (pruritus) and/or skin rash ('nettle rash' or hives) with no change in vital signs. They are most common in patients receiving plasma-rich components such as FFP or platelets.

Symptoms often improve if the transfusion is slowed and an antihistamine (e.g. chlorpheniramine) is administered orally or intravenously. The patient must be monitored closely for development of a more severe reaction, in which case the transfusion must be stopped.

Several studies, including randomised controlled trials, have shown no benefit for routine pre-medication with antihistamines or steroids. Patients with recurrent mild allergic reactions who respond poorly to slowing the transfusion and administering an antihistamine should be discussed with a specialist in transfusion medicine or allergy. They may be considered for a trial of washed components. The possibility of other causes, such as latex allergy or drug reaction, should also be considered.

## 5.2.4 Delayed transfusion reactions

### 5.2.4.1 Delayed haemolytic transfusion reactions (DHTRs)

DHTRs occur more than 24 hours after transfusion in a patient who has previously been 'alloimmunised' to a red cell antigen by blood transfusion or pregnancy. The antibody may have fallen to a level that is undetectable by the pre-transfusion antibody screen and the patient is then inadvertently re-exposed to red cells of the immunising group. Antibodies to the Kidd (Jk) blood group system are the most common cause of DHTRs reported to SHOT, followed by antibodies to Rh antigens.

Transfusion of antigen-positive red cells causes a boost in the patient's antibody levels (secondary immune response) leading to haemolysis of the transfused cells. Haemolysis becomes clinically apparent up to 14 days after the transfusion and signs may include a falling Hb concentration or failure to achieve the expected increment, jaundice, fever and occasionally haemoglobinuria or acute renal failure. Delayed reactions may be missed, especially if the patient has been discharged. In sickle cell disease, the clinical features of a DHTR may be misdiagnosed as a sickle cell crisis.

Clinical suspicion of DHTRs should be confirmed by laboratory investigations including blood count and reticulocytes, examination of the blood film, plasma bilirubin, renal function tests and LDH. Serological investigations should include repeat blood group and antibody screen (on pre- and post-transfusion patient samples), DAT and elution of antibodies from the patient's red cells for identification.

Treatment of DHTRs is usually supportive, sometimes requiring further transfusion. The offending antibodies must be recorded on the transfusion laboratory computer and medical records and patients are usually issued with an 'Antibody Card' to carry and present to clinical staff whenever further transfusion is required. Patients investigated by Blood Services reference laboratories will also have their antibodies recorded on a central database. All DHTRs should be reported to SHOT and the MHRA.

### 5.2.4.2 Transfusion-associated graft-versus-host disease (TA-GvHD)

This rare and almost always fatal complication occurs when viable lymphocytes in a blood donation engraft in the patient and mount an immune response against the recipient's cells of a different HLA type. At-risk patients usually have impaired cell-mediated immunity and are unable to reject the foreign cells. These include fetuses receiving intrauterine transfusion, patients with inherited immunodeficiency disorders affecting T-cell function, medical procedures causing very severe immunosuppression such as allogeneic stem cell transplantation or treatment with specific chemotherapy drugs such as purine analogues. TA-GvHD has occasionally been reported in non-immunosuppressed patients receiving a blood transfusion from an HLA-matched donor or a close relative with HLA types in common. Patients receiving conventional combination chemotherapy for cancer are not at increased risk of TA-GvHD and it has not been reported in HIV positive transfusion recipients. Clinical aspects of TA-GvHD prevention in haemato-oncology patients and neonates/infants are discussed in Chapters 8 and 10 respectively.

Symptoms classically occur 7 to 14 days (maximum 30 days) after transfusion with fever, skin rash, diarrhoea, disturbed liver function and worsening bone marrow aplasia. Diagnosis is based on showing the typical features of acute GvHD in biopsies of affected organs and demonstration of donor-derived cells or DNA in the patient's blood or tissues. The UK Blood Services provide specialist diagnostic services. Only one case of TA-GvHD has been reported in the UK since 2000 (an intrauterine transfusion of non-irradiated maternal blood). Routine leucodepletion of blood components has clearly reduced the risk of TA-GvHD but it remains essential to ensure that all at-risk patients receive irradiated red cells or platelet components. The BCSH *Guidelines on the Use of Irradiated Blood Components* (http://www.bcshguidelines.com) regularly update the list of patients and therapeutic agents that require the use of irradiated blood components in the light of current research.

### 5.2.4.3 Post-transfusion purpura (PTP)

Affected individuals develop a very low platelet count and bleeding 5 to 12 days after transfusion of red cells. The typical patient is a parous female who is negative for a common platelet antigen, most commonly HPA-1a, and may have been initially sensitised by carrying a HPA-1a positive fetus in pregnancy. PTP is caused by re-stimulation of platelet-specific alloantibodies in the patient that also damage their own (antigen-negative) platelets by an 'innocent bystander' reaction. This severe, and potentially fatal, complication has become rare since the introduction of leucodepleted blood components.

Advice in diagnosis and management should be sought from transfusion medicine specialists and Blood Service laboratories. Platelet transfusions are usually ineffective (but may be given in high doses in patients with life-threatening bleeding) but most patients show a prompt and sustained response to high-dose intravenous immunoglobulin (IVIg).

# 5.3   Infectious hazards of transfusion

Historically, transfusion-transmitted infections (TTIs) dominated the transfusion safety agenda but they are now rare in developed countries. However, constant vigilance is required to counter the risk from established and newly emergent pathogens in the era of mass international travel. Novel transfusion-transmissible agents, such as prions, have also emerged to threaten the safety of the blood supply.

## 5.3.1   Viral infections

With modern donor selection and testing, hepatitis B, hepatitis C and HIV transmission are now very rare in the UK (Table 5.3). The current risk of an infectious donation entering the UK blood supply is now <1 in 1.2 million donations for hepatitis B, <1 in 7 million for HIV and <1 in 28 million for hepatitis C.

With the exception of hepatitis B, conventional screening tests were traditionally based on the detection of viral antibodies in donor blood. There is a small risk of infectious products entering the blood supply if a donation is made during the window period early in the course of infection before a detectable antibody response. These window periods have been much reduced by the addition of antigen testing and nucleic acid testing (NAT). Donations from new donors carry a slightly higher risk of viral positivity than repeat (previously tested) donors. Table 5.4 summarises the 23 confirmed viral transmissions (28 affected recipients) reported to the UK Blood Services between 1996 and 2012.

**Table 5.3 Estimated risk per million blood donations of hepatitis B virus, hepatitis C virus and HIV entering the blood supply due to the window period of tests in use, UK 2010–2012 (data and information collected by the NHSBT/Public Health England Epidemiology Unit)**

|  | Hepatitis B virus | Hepatitis C virus | HIV |
|---|---|---|---|
| All donations | 0.79 | 0.035 | 0.14 |
| Donation from repeat donors | 0.65 | 0.025 | 0.14 |
| Donations from new donors | 2.23 | 0.133 | 0.18 |

**Table 5.4** Confirmed viral transfusion-transmitted infections, number of infected recipients and outcomes reported to UK Blood Services 1996–2012 (extracted from SHOT Annual Report 2012)

| Infection | No. of incidents | No. of infected recipients | Deaths related to infection | Major morbidity | Minor morbidity |
|---|---|---|---|---|---|
| Hepatitis A | 3 | 3 | 0 | 2 | 1 |
| Hepatitis B | 11 | 13 | 0 | 13 | 0 |
| Hepatitis C | 2 | 2 | 0 | 2 | 0 |
| Hepatitis E | 2 | 3 | 0 | 1 | 2 |
| HIV | 2 | 4 | 0 | 4 | 0 |
| HTLV | 2 | 2 | 0 | 2 | 0 |
| Parvovirus B19 | 1 | 1 | 0 | 1 | 0 |

### 5.3.1.1  Hepatitis A

This is primarily an acute enteric infection spread by the faeco-oral route (contaminated food or water). Transmission by transfusion is very rare as affected individuals are usually unwell and deferred from donation. There is no carrier state and blood donations are not screened for hepatitis A antibody or antigen. As a non-enveloped virus it is resistant to methods of pathogen inactivation such as solvent detergent treatment.

### 5.3.1.2  Hepatitis B

The hepatitis B virus (HBV) is readily transmitted by infectious blood or body fluids, including sexual intercourse and parenteral drug use, and perinatal transmission is common in endemic areas such as the Far East and China. Most patients recover after the initial episode of acute hepatitis but some develop a chronic carrier state, estimated at 350 million individuals worldwide, with long-term risk of cirrhosis of the liver and hepatocellular cancer. Hepatitis B remains the most commonly reported viral TTI in the UK because of window period transmissions but more sensitive screening tests for blood donations, such as HBV NAT, are increasingly effective.

### 5.3.1.3  Hepatitis C

There are around 170 million affected individuals worldwide. Initial infection is often symptomless but around 80% of patients develop a chronic carrier state with long-term risk of cirrhosis, liver failure and liver cancer. Hepatitis C was formerly a major cause of TTI, known as 'non-A non-B hepatitis', but the risk of transmission by blood transfusion has fallen dramatically since the introduction of antibody screening in 1991 and progressively more sensitive tests for hepatitis C antigen and RNA since 1999.

### 5.3.1.4  Hepatitis E

Caused by a small non-enveloped RNA virus, hepatitis E was formerly believed to be most prevalent in warmer climates and less developed countries where it is mainly spread by the faeco-oral route. In Western countries, recent studies have indicated large numbers of asymptomatic infections and up to 13% of individuals in England are seropositive for hepatitis E antibodies. Hepatitis E usually produces a self-limiting acute hepatitis but can lead to chronic infection, especially in immunocompromised patients, and may cause cirrhosis of the liver. An increase in the frequency of diagnoses of hepatitis E in patients in the UK has been seen in recent years. Transmission by blood transfusion has been confirmed with single UK cases reported to SHOT in 2004 and 2012. Blood Services are monitoring the situation closely, and working to establish the risk to transfusion recipients.

### 5.3.1.5  Human immunodeficiency virus (HIV) 1 and 2

Transfusion transmission by both single-donor and pooled blood components was common early in the course of the 1980s epidemic of acquired immunodeficiency syndrome (AIDS). Modern donor selection and screening has made transmission a rare event in the UK. The two incidents identified since SHOT reporting began (1996 and 2003) were both from HIV antibody negative window period donations before the introduction of HIV RNA screening.

### 5.3.1.6  Cytomegalovirus (CMV)

Cytomegalovirus is a common herpes virus that causes asymptomatic infection or a mild glandular fever-like illness in most healthy individuals. Despite an antibody response (seroconversion), the virus persists in blood monocytes and 50–60% of adults in the UK, including blood donors, are lifelong carriers of the virus. It can be transmitted by transfusion of cellular blood components although this may be difficult to distinguish from reactivation of previous infection. CMV can cause severe, sometimes fatal, infection in fetuses, neonates and immunocompromised adults. There has long been debate about the relative merits of donor CMV antibody screening (CMV negative components) or routine pre-storage leucodepletion in preventing transmission to patients at risk. In 2012, the Advisory Committee on the Safety of Blood, Tissues and Organs (SaBTO) produced an evidence-based position statement (http://www.dh.gov.uk/prod_consum_dh/groups/dh_digitalassets/@dh/@en/documents/digitalasset/dh_133086.pdf). This can be summarised as follows:

- CMV seronegative red cells and platelets should be provided for intrauterine transfusions and neonates (up to 28 days after expected date of delivery).
- CMV seronegative granulocytes should be provided for CMV seronegative recipients.
- CMV seronegative red cells and platelets should be provided, where possible, for pregnant women. In an emergency, such as major haemorrhage, standard leucocyte-depleted components should be given to avoid delay.
- Standard pre-storage leucodepleted components are suitable for all other transfusion recipients, including haemopoietic stem cell transplant patients, organ transplant patients and immune deficient patients, including those with HIV.

### 5.3.1.7  Human T-cell lymphotropic virus types I and II (HTLV I and II)

These T-cell-associated RNA retroviruses are endemic in southwest Japan, the Caribbean Basin, sub-Saharan Africa and parts of South America, where they affect 15–20 million people. They are transmitted by sexual contact, breastfeeding, shared needles and blood transfusion. The clinical significance of HTLV II is uncertain but HTLV I is associated with a 1 to 4% lifetime risk of developing adult T-cell leukaemia/lymphoma (ATLL) or the chronic neurological disease HTLV I related myelopathy (HAM) many decades after infection. The combination of donor screening for antibodies to HTLV I and II plus leucodepletion of cellular blood components has virtually eliminated transmission by transfusion in the UK.

### 5.3.1.8 Human parvovirus B19 (HPV B19)

Infection with this common, seasonal, non-enveloped DNA virus is often asymptomatic and there is no chronic carrier state. It causes the childhood illness erythema infectiosum ('slapped cheek syndrome'). Transient infection of red cell precursors in the marrow can cause an aplastic crisis in patients with shortened red cell survival such as sickle cell disease, thalassaemia major and chronic haemolytic anaemias. Infection of non-immune mothers in the second trimester of pregnancy may cause severe anaemia (hydrops fetalis) or death of the fetus. The virus can be transmitted by cellular blood components or frozen plasma and is resistant to pathogen inactivation techniques such as solvent detergent treatment. Although routine blood donor testing is not performed, only one TTI was reported to SHOT between 1996 and 2012. Products manufactured from large donor plasma pools, such as immunoglobulins and clotting factor concentrates, are screened for high titres of HPV B19 RNA.

### 5.3.1.9 West Nile Virus (WNV)

This mosquito-borne flavivirus has spread from its traditional distribution in Africa, western Asia, southern Europe and Australia in recent years and now produces seasonal epidemics across the United States and Canada, usually between May and November. Most infections are mild or asymptomatic, but around 0.5% of patients develop severe encephalitis that may be fatal. Blood donors may transmit the infection during the 3- to 15-day incubation period; therefore, individuals returning from affected areas are deferred from donation for 28 days or may be accepted for donation with the added precaution of WNV NAT screening.

## 5.3.2 Bacterial infections

### 5.3.2.1 Syphilis

All donations are routinely screened for antibodies to *Treponema pallidum*. Transmission is now extremely rare and no cases have been reported since SHOT surveillance began in 1996.

### 5.3.2.2 Other bacterial infections

Blood components may be contaminated by bacteria, most often derived from the donor arm at the time of collection, which can proliferate on storage and harm the recipient. Bacteria from the normal skin flora, such as the coagulase negative staphylococci rarely produce severe infections although febrile reactions may occur. More pathogenic gram positive bacteria, such as *Staphylococcus aureus*, and gram negatives, such as *E. coli*, *Klebsiella* spp. and *Pseudomonas* spp., may produce life-threatening reactions. Between 1996 and 2012, 40 acute transfusion reactions due to confirmed bacterial transmission were reported to SHOT, affecting 43 recipients, of whom 11 died. Thirty-three of these transmissions were from platelet packs and seven were from red cells.

Bacterial TTIs are more common with platelet components because of their storage at 20–24°C. The risk increases with storage time after donation and is the main reason for the short shelf life of platelet components. Platelet donors often give two or more adult therapeutic doses at a single apheresis session, with the risk of an infected donation affecting multiple recipients. Up to 1 in 2000 platelet packs contain detectable bacteria 5 days after donation and fatal reactions have been reported in 1 in 25000–80000 transfusions. By contrast, most pathogenic bacteria grow poorly in refrigerated red cell components although some gram negative organisms, such as *Yersinia enterocolitica* and *Pseudomonas* spp., can proliferate in these conditions.

### 5.3.2.3 Preventing bacterial transmission

Improved techniques for cleaning/decontamination of the donor arm and diversion of the first 20–30 mL of the donation into a side-pouch (this blood is used for donor testing) have produced a marked fall in the reports of bacterial TTIs in the UK. No cases were reported to SHOT between 2009 and 2012. As an additional safety measure, the UK Blood Services have introduced automated culture of all platelet donations and this may allow the safe extension of their shelf life from 5 to 7 days.

Pathogen inactivation (PI) technologies for platelets and red cells, such as the use of light-activated psoralens that kill organisms by damaging their DNA or RNA, are being developed and have the potential to eliminate both bacterial and viral TTIs. At present, the cost-effectiveness of PI is uncertain and early clinical studies of the currently licensed system have raised concerns about its effect on platelet function.

## 5.3.3 Protozoal infections

### 5.3.3.1 Malaria

Despite increasing international travel, transfusion-transmitted malaria remains a rare event in the UK. There have been two cases reported to SHOT (both *Plasmodium falciparum*) since 1996, the last in 2003, one of which was fatal. A policy of taking a travel history at the time of donation combined with deferral and, where indicated, testing for malarial antibodies has proved effective.

### 5.3.3.2 Chagas disease

This serious multi-system disease, caused by *Trypanosoma cruzi*, is endemic in Central and South America and may be transmitted by blood transfusion. No transfusion-transmitted cases have been recorded in the UK and precautions centre on donor history of residence/travel and, where appropriate, testing for antibodies to the parasite.

# 5.4 Variant Creutzfeldt–Jakob disease (vCJD)

This fatal neurological disease, due to the same agent (abnormal variant of prion protein) as bovine spongiform encephalopathy (BSE) in cattle and caused by eating beef from affected animals, was first identified in the UK in 1996. By the end of 2012 there had been 174 cases in the UK, peaking in 2000. Four cases of transfusion-transmitted vCJD infection have been identified, from three apparently healthy donors who later developed vCJD. All occurred with non-leucodepleted red cells donated before 1999. Three of the four recipients died of vCJD a few years after the implicated transfusion. The fourth recipient died of unrelated causes but had abnormal prion protein in the spleen at post-mortem examination (significance uncertain). There are still many uncertainties around the pathogenesis and epidemiology of vCJD and no practical screening test for blood donors has yet been developed. The vCJD risk-reduction measures introduced in the UK include (see also Chapter 3):

■ Importation of plasma for fractionated blood products (1998)
■ Leucodepletion of all blood components (1999)
■ Importation (and viral inactivation) of fresh frozen plasma for all patients born on or after 1 January 1996 (when dietary transmission of vCJD is assumed to have ceased) (2002)

■ Exclusion of blood donors who have received a blood transfusion in the UK since 1980 (2004)
■ Importation of solvent detergent plasma for adult patients undergoing plasma exchange for thrombotic thrombocytopenic purpura (2006).

The efficacy and safety of prion filters for blood components has been investigated but their cost-effectiveness is uncertain as the numbers of clinical cases of vCJD have reduced. There is also interest in the cohort of individuals born after measures to eliminate contaminated beef products from the UK diet were instituted in 1996 ('class of 96') who are becoming eligible to donate blood as they reach the age of 17.

# 6

# ALTERNATIVES AND ADJUNCTS TO BLOOD TRANSFUSION

# Essentials

- Transfusion alternatives were mostly developed to reduce blood use in surgery but have much wider application.
- They are most effective when used in combination and as part of a comprehensive patient blood management programme.
- Predeposit autologous blood donation before surgery is of uncertain benefit and now has very restricted indications in the UK.
- Intraoperative cell salvage (ICS) is effective (and may be life-saving) in elective or emergency high blood loss surgery and management of major haemorrhage.
- Postoperative cell salvage (PCS) and reinfusion can reduce blood use in joint replacement and scoliosis surgery.
- ICS and PCS are usually acceptable to Jehovah's Witnesses.
- Tranexamic acid (antifibrinolytic) is inexpensive, safe and reduces mortality in traumatic haemorrhage. It reduces bleeding and transfusion in many surgical procedures and may be effective in obstetric and gastrointestinal haemorrhage.
- Off-label use of recombinant activated Factor VII (rFVIIa) for haemorrhage does not reduce mortality and can cause serious thromboembolic complications.
- Erythropoiesis stimulating agents (ESAs), such as erythropoietin, are standard therapy in renal anaemia and can support blood conservation in some cancer chemotherapy patients and autologous blood donation programmes. They may also be effective in selected patients with myelodysplasia.
- ESAs may cause hypertension and thromboembolic problems. Careful monitoring is required to keep the haematocrit below 35%.
- Safe parenteral iron preparations are now available and may produce more rapid and complete responses in iron deficiency anaemia. Indications include intolerance of oral iron, support for ESA therapy and as an alternative to transfusion in perioperative and postpartum anaemia.

Transfusion alternatives have largely been developed to reduce donor red cell transfusion in surgery, where they are most effective as part of a comprehensive 'patient blood management' programme (see Chapter 7). Many of these techniques have wider application, ranging from traumatic and obstetric haemorrhage to patients who do not accept blood transfusions. This chapter briefly describes the commonly available transfusion alternatives and their rationale. Their use in specific clinical indications is covered in Chapters 7–10 and 12.

# 6.1 Autologous blood transfusion (collection and reinfusion of the patient's own red blood cells)

## 6.1.1 Predeposit autologous donation (PAD)

This is the banking of red cell units from the patient before planned surgery.

PAD was stimulated by concerns about viral transmission by donor blood, especially during the HIV epidemic of the early 1980s. With a red cell storage-life of 35 days at 4°C, most healthy adult patients can donate up to three red cell units before elective surgery. Patients may be given iron supplements, sometimes with erythropoietin, to prevent anaemia or allow more donations to be collected. The Blood Safety and Quality Regulations (BSQR, 2005) require that donations for PAD must be performed in a licensed blood establishment, rather than a routine hospital setting. The donations must be processed and tested in the same way as donor blood and are subject to the same requirements for traceability.

Given the current remote risk of viral transfusion-transmitted infection by donor blood in developed countries, the rationale, safety and cost-effectiveness of routine PAD has been severely questioned (see 2007 British Committee for Standards in Haematology (BCSH) *Guidelines for Policies on Alternatives to Allogeneic Blood Transfusion. 1. Predeposit Autologous Blood Donation and Transfusion* – http://www.bcshguidelines.com) and the procedure is now rarely performed in the UK. Although PAD may reduce exposure to donor blood, it does not reduce overall exposure to transfusion procedures or protect against wrong blood into patient episodes due to identification errors at collection from the blood bank or at the bedside. Indeed, the availability of autologous blood may increase the risk of unnecessary transfusion. Most Jehovah's Witnesses will decline PAD (see Chapter 12). Clinical trials of PAD are mainly small and of low quality and do not provide strong evidence that the risks outweigh the benefits. The BCSH guideline on PAD only recommends its use in 'exceptional circumstances', and lists the following indications for PAD:

- Patients with rare blood groups or multiple blood group antibodies where compatible allogeneic (donor) blood is difficult to obtain.
- Patients at serious psychiatric risk because of anxiety about exposure to donor blood.
- Patients who refuse to consent to donor blood transfusion but will accept PAD.
- Children undergoing scoliosis surgery (in practice, most specialist units now use other blood conservation measures).

PAD should only be considered in surgery with a significant likelihood of requiring transfusion, operation dates must be guaranteed and the patient's ability to donate safely must be assessed by a 'competent clinician', usually a transfusion medicine specialist. Adverse events and reactions associated with PAD (or other autologous transfusion systems) should be reported to the Serious Hazards of Transfusion (SHOT) haemovigilance scheme and the Medicines and Healthcare Products Regulatory Agency (MHRA).

## 6.1.2   Intraoperative cell salvage (ICS)

This is the collection and reinfusion of blood spilled during surgery.

Commercially available, largely automated devices are available for ICS and are now widely used in hospitals for both elective and emergency surgery with significant blood loss and in the management of major traumatic or obstetric haemorrhage. The machines must always be used and maintained according to the manufacturer's instructions by appropriately trained staff. A 2010 Cochrane Collaboration review of randomised trials of ICS, mainly in cardiac and orthopaedic surgery, showed a 20% reduction in donor blood exposure (an average saving of 0.7 units per patient). Much useful information about clinical indications and use of ICS, policies for implementation, staff training/competency assessment and patient information has been prepared by the UK Cell Salvage Action Group (UKCSAG) (http://www.transfusionguidelines.org.uk/Index.aspx?Publication=BBT&Section=22&pageid=7507).

Blood lost into the surgical field is aspirated into a collection reservoir after filtration to remove particulate debris. It is then anticoagulated with heparin or citrate. If sufficient blood is collected and the patient loses sufficient blood to require transfusion, the salvaged blood can be centrifuged and washed in a closed, automated system. Red cells suspended in sterile saline solution are produced, which must be transfused to the patient within 4 hours of processing. The reinfusion bag should be labelled **in the operating theatre** with the minimum patient identifiers derived from the patient's ID band (UKCSAG has developed a suitable label for this purpose). The red cells are transfused through a 200 μm screen filter, as in a standard blood administration set, except in those instances where a leucodepletion filter is indicated (see below). The transfusion should be prescribed, documented and the patient monitored in the same way as for any transfusion. Patients undergoing elective procedures where ICS may be used should give informed consent after provision of relevant information.

Indications for ICS in adults and children (for whom low-volume processing bowls are available) are as follows:

- Surgery where the anticipated blood loss is >20% of the patient's estimated blood volume.
- Elective or emergency surgery in patients with risk factors for bleeding (including high-risk Caesarean section) or low preoperative Hb concentration.
- Major haemorrhage.
- Patients with rare blood groups or multiple blood group antibodies for whom it may be difficult to provide donor blood.
- Patients who do not accept donor blood transfusions but are prepared to accept, and consent to, ICS (this includes most Jehovah's Witnesses).

ICS should not be used when bowel contents contaminate the operation site and blood should not be aspirated from bacterially infected surgical fields.

Because of concerns about cancer cell reinfusion and spread, manufacturers do not recommend ICS in patients having surgery for malignant disease. However, extensive clinical experience suggests this is not a significant risk although it is recommended to reinfuse the red cells through a leucodepletion filter.

ICS is now widely used in women at high risk of postpartum haemorrhage during Caesarean section and in the management of major obstetric haemorrhage and is supported by many specialist and national guideline groups (http://guidance.nice.org.uk/IPG144/). Theoretical concerns about amniotic fluid embolism have not been borne out in practice, although gross fluid contamination should be aspirated before blood collection and the harvested red cells should be reinfused through a leucodepletion filter.

### 6.1.3 Postoperative cell salvage (PCS)

PCS is mainly used in orthopaedic procedures, especially after knee or hip replacement and in correction of scoliosis. Blood is collected from wound drains and then either filtered or washed in an automated system before reinfusion to the patient.

The simple filtration systems for reinfusion of unwashed red cells are mainly used when expected blood losses are between 500 and 1000 mL. With these infusion volumes concerns about adverse effects on blood coagulation have not been confirmed in routine practice. Clinical staff must be trained and competency assessed to use the device, accurately document the collection and label the pack at the bedside. Collection of salvaged blood must be completed within the manufacturer's specified time (usually 6 hours) and the reinfusion must be monitored and documented in the same way as donor transfusions.

PCS is relatively cheap, has the potential to reduce exposure to donor blood and is acceptable to most Jehovah's Witnesses. It remains unclear whether it adds significantly to a comprehensive blood conservation programme which includes preoperative optimisation of Hb, haemostatic/antifibrinolytic measures during surgery and strict postoperative transfusion thresholds.

### 6.1.4   Acute normovolaemic haemodilution (ANH)

In ANH several units of blood are collected into standard blood donation packs immediately before surgery (usually in the operating room) and the patient's blood volume is maintained by the simultaneous infusion of crystalloid or colloid fluids. The blood is stored in the operating theatre at room temperature and reinfused at the end of surgery or if significant bleeding occurs. ANH is most often used in cardiac bypass surgery where the immediate postoperative transfusion of 'fresh whole blood' containing platelets and clotting factors is seen as an advantage. Reported hazards of ANH include fluid overload, cardiac ischemia and wrong blood into patient errors. Mathematical modelling suggests ANH is most effective as a blood conservation measure in surgery with major blood loss – now uncommon in elective cardiac surgery. Systematic reviews of published trials have found no significant reduction in exposure to donor transfusions compared to standard care or other blood conservation techniques and the safety of ANH remains unclear.

# 6.2   Pharmacological measures to reduce transfusion

## 6.2.1   Antifibrinolytic and procoagulant drugs

### 6.2.1.1   Tranexamic acid

Tranexamic acid, a synthetic lysine derivative, inhibits fibrinolysis (the breakdown of blood clots) by reducing the conversion of plasmin to plasminogen. It is low cost and can be used by the oral or intravenous route. It is closely related to, but more potent than, the older agent $\Sigma$ aminocaproic acid (EACA).

A recent systematic review of trials in many forms of surgery confirms that tranexamic acid reduces both the risk of receiving a blood transfusion (by around 30%) and the need for further surgery due to re-bleeding. A small increase in the risk of thromboembolic events could not be excluded but there was no increase in mortality in patients receiving tranexamic acid. Many different dosages were used in surgical trials, but low-dose protocols appeared equally effective (see the list below).

The international CRASH-2 randomised trial of more than 20 000 patients with major traumatic haemorrhage showed a significant reduction in mortality in patients receiving tranexamic acid within 3 hours of trauma and there was no increase in thromboembolic events (including patients with traumatic brain injury). A major international trial of tranexamic acid in 15 000 women with major postpartum haemorrhage (the WOMAN trial) is being conducted and trials are also in progress in gastrointestinal haemorrhage.

In view of these findings, many experts agree that tranexamic acid should be included in major traumatic haemorrhage protocols and may safely be used in most surgical blood conservation programmes.

Examples of published tranexamic acid doses are as follows:

- Cardiac surgery: 10 mg/kg intravenously (IV) immediately pre-op followed by IV infusion of 1 mg/kg/h.
- Traumatic haemorrhage in adults (CRASH-2): 1 g IV within 3 hours of the event followed by 1 g infused over 8 hours.
- Traumatic haemorrhage in children: 15 mL/kg (maximum 1000 mg) IV over 10 minutes followed by 2 mg/kg/h (max 125 mg/h) by IV infusion until haemorrhage is controlled.
- Postpartum haemorrhage (WOMAN trial): 1 g IV followed by a further 1g if bleeding continues or recurs.

## 6.2.2  Aprotinin

Aprotinin inhibits many proteolytic enzymes and reduces fibrinolysis. It is bovine in origin and severe allergic reactions, occasionally fatal, occur in up to 1 in 200 patients on first exposure. Repeat administration is not advised within 12 months. Aprotinin is mainly used in cardiac surgery where it appears to be more effective than tranexamic acid in reducing blood loss and blood transfusion. However, several retrospective studies have shown an increase in thromboembolic events, renal failure and overall mortality compared to other antifibrinolytic drugs. It was temporarily withdrawn from prescription in 2007 and is now recommended for use only in those patients with a particularly high risk of bleeding in whom the benefits are believed to exceed the risks. Aprotinin is significantly more expensive than tranexamic acid.

## 6.2.3  Tissue sealants

Also known as 'biological glues' or 'tissue adhesives', tissue sealants may be derived from human or animal clotting factors such as fibrinogen (sometimes activated by thrombin in the syringe immediately before administration) or synthetic hydrogel polymers. They are sprayed on surgical fields or raw surfaces to promote haemostasis and reduce blood loss. Clinical trials show that they can reduce surgical bleeding and exposure to donor blood, the effect being most significant in orthopaedic surgery.

## 6.2.4  Recombinant activated Factor VII (rFVIIa, NovoSeven™)

rFVIIa directly activates blood-clot formation at sites of exposed tissue factor in damaged blood vessels, bypassing other clotting pathways. It is only licensed for the treatment of bleeding in patients with haemophilia A or B with inhibitors. However, more than 95% of its use worldwide is off label in patients with major haemorrhage or as 'last ditch' treatment in bleeding refractory to other treatment. The main off-label uses are in cardiac surgery, trauma, intracranial haemorrhage and liver/abdominal surgery. It is an extremely expensive drug and the appropriate dose for non-haemophilia bleeding is unknown. Acidosis, common in major traumatic haemorrhage, reduces its effectiveness and adequate levels of fibrinogen are needed for clot formation.

Reports of the effectiveness of off-label rFVIIa are distorted by positive publication bias – mainly case reports of spectacular results and small, underpowered trials. Registry studies are less encouraging. They show little, if any, reduction in mortality and a significant incidence of serious venous and arterial thromboembolic events, especially in older patients and those with vascular disease. A recent Cochrane Collaboration systematic review of randomised controlled trials of prophylactic or therapeutic rFVIIa in patients without haemophilia also found no evidence of reduced mortality and, at the most, a modest reduction in blood loss or transfusion (http://onlinelibrary.wiley.com/doi/10.1002/14651858.CD005011.pub4/abstract).

Higher doses were no more effective and it is not a substitute for coagulation factor replacement. In view of this, the routine use of rFVIIa for non-haemophilia bleeding cannot be recommended outside well-designed clinical trials, and hospitals should have clear local protocols for its use (or not) in emergency settings.

## 6.2.5 Desmopressin (DDAVP)

Desmopressin causes the release of Factor VIIIc and von Willebrand factor (vWF) from endothelial cells and is used to treat or prevent bleeding in patients with mild type I von Willebrand's disease or haemophilia A. It may reduce bleeding in patients with uraemia and platelet dysfunction due to kidney failure. The standard dose for this indication is 0.3 µg/kg subcutaneously or intravenously. The template bleeding time is shortened within 60 minutes and the effect lasts less than 24 hours. Repeat doses may be less effective as stores of vWF are depleted. It may also cause headaches and facial flushing.

## 6.2.6 Erythropoiesis stimulating agents (ESAs)

Erythropoietin (Epo) is produced in the kidneys and increases red blood cell production in the bone marrow in response to reduced oxygen delivery to the tissues. Recombinant human erythropoietin (rHuEpo) was initially licensed for treating the anaemia of renal failure and longer-acting forms, such as darbopoietin alfa, have now been introduced. Other licensed indications include treating anaemia and reducing transfusion requirements in some cancer patients undergoing chemotherapy, increasing the yield of blood in PAD programmes and reducing exposure to donor blood in adults undergoing major orthopaedic surgery. Some patients with 'low-risk' myelodysplasia have also been successfully treated with rHuEpo off-label. ESAs are expensive and more research is needed to develop guidelines for their use in combination with other blood conservation measures.

**Table 6.1 Licensed indications and summary of dosage recommendations for the major erythropoiesis stimulating agents used in blood conservation**

| ESA | Licensed (non-renal) indications | Recommended dose |
|---|---|---|
| Epoietin alfa | Treatment of anaemia and reduction of transfusion in adult patients receiving chemotherapy for solid tumours, lymphoma or myeloma | Initial dose (subcutaneous injection): 150 IU/kg 3 times weekly or 450 IU/kg once weekly |
| | Preoperative autologous donation (of up to four units collected over 3 weeks) | 600 IU/kg intravenous 2 times weekly for 3 weeks prior to surgery |
| | Prior to major orthopaedic surgery in adults | 600 IU/kg subcutaneously on days −21, −14, −7 and day of surgery |
| Epoietin beta | Symptomatic anaemia in adult patients with non-myeloid malignancies receiving chemotherapy | Initial dose (subcutaneous injection) 30 000 IU once weekly (approximately 450 IU/kg) |
| | Preoperative autologous donation | 2 times weekly for 4 weeks by subcutaneous or intravenous injection using manufacturer's algorithm for dosing (see SPC) |
| Darbopoietin alfa | Symptomatic anaemia in adult cancer patients with non-myeloid malignancies receiving chemotherapy | Initial dose 500 µg (6.75 µg/kg) subcutaneously once every 3 weeks |

Higher haematocrits may cause thromboembolic complications. Guidelines recommend that a haematocrit of 35% (Hb approximately 120 g/L) should not be exceeded. ESAs may also increase the risk of tumour growth or recurrence in certain cancers. There have been rare cases of pure red cell aplasia associated with rHuEpo treatment.

The dosage, scheduling and licensed indications for use in blood conservation vary between different ESAs (Table 6.1) and prescribers should refer to the current Summary of Product Characteristics (SPC) for each preparation, the British National Formulary and expert haematological and pharmacological advice when developing local protocols. It is usually necessary to co-administer oral or intravenous iron with Epo to support the increase in red cell production.

## 6.3 Thrombopoietin mimetics

These increase platelet production by stimulating the receptor for the hormone thrombopoietin (THPO). Romiplastin (Nplate™) is given by subcutaneous injection and Eltrombopag (Promacta®) is an oral agent. Both are licensed for the treatment of idiopathic thrombocytopenic purpura (ITP). Research is in progress to assess their ability to prevent bleeding and reduce platelet transfusions in aplastic anaemia, myelodysplasia and chemotherapy-induced thrombocytopenia. Early encouraging results are tempered by concerns about a possible increased risk of thromboembolic events, bone marrow fibrosis and a theoretical risk of stimulating malignant cells. Therefore, these agents should only be used off-label in the context of clinical trials.

## 6.4 Parenteral iron

Oral iron is the preferred, and safest, first-line therapy for most patients with iron deficiency anaemia but many users experience gastrointestinal side effects and compliance with treatment is poor. In patients receiving ESA, oral iron replacement is often inadequate and 'functional iron deficiency' limits the response to treatment. Parenteral iron produces more rapid responses and better repletion of iron stores in several clinical settings but, until recently, its use was limited by a significant risk of severe, occasionally fatal, allergic reactions with the available preparations (especially high molecular weight iron dextran). The currently available preparations have a very low incidence of serious reactions and have brought parenteral iron back into mainstream practice. Common indications for the use of intravenous iron include:

- Iron deficiency anaemia with intolerance of oral iron, especially in inflammatory bowel disease, or where oral iron is ineffective.
- To support the use of erythropoiesis stimulating agents (including patients on renal dialysis).
- As an alternative to blood transfusion when a rapid increase in Hb is required (e.g. perioperative anaemia, severe anaemia in late pregnancy or postpartum anaemia).

Several parenteral iron preparations are now licensed in the UK. Some, such as iron sucrose (Venofer®), are given up to three times weekly by slow intravenous injection or short infusion and may need several weeks of treatment for a full replacement dose to be administered. Others, such as low molecular weight iron dextrans (Cosmofer®), may be given as a single total dose infusion over several hours. More recently introduced agents, such as ferric carboxymaltose (Ferinject®) or iron isomaltoside (Monofer®) have the advantage of administering large replacement doses more rapidly (15 to 60 minutes).

The newer preparations are more expensive and clinical experience is still limited. Parenteral iron is contraindicated in the first trimester of pregnancy. The availability of individual parenteral iron preparations varies between hospitals and they should be used according to local guidelines and policies. Detailed information about dose and administration is available in the individual Summary of Product Characteristics and the British National Formulary (http://bnf.org/bnf).

# EFFECTIVE TRANSFUSION IN SURGERY AND CRITICAL CARE

# Essentials

- Transfusion of blood according to evidence-based guidelines improves patient safety and conserves precious blood supplies.
- The decision to transfuse should be based on clinical assessment as well as laboratory tests.
- The use of red cells in surgery has decreased but audits show many transfusions are inappropriate and there is wide variation in practice between clinical teams.
- Patient blood management programmes to improve surgical transfusion work across primary and secondary care and focus on:
  - preoperative optimisation
  - minimising blood loss at surgery
  - avoiding unnecessary transfusion after surgery
  - using blood conservation techniques (e.g. intraoperative cell salvage) and transfusion alternatives (e.g. antifibrinolytic drugs) where appropriate.
- Restrictive red cell transfusion strategies are safe in a wide variety of surgeries and in critical care patients.
- In the haemodynamically stable, non-bleeding patient transfusion should only be considered if the Hb is 80 g/L or less. A single red cell unit (or equivalent weight-related dose in children) may be transfused and the patient reassessed.
- Most invasive surgical procedures can be carried out safely with a platelet count above $50 \times 10^9$/L or international normalised ratio (INR) below 2.0.
- Successful transfusion support in major haemorrhage depends on the rapid provision of compatible blood, a protocol-driven multidisciplinary team approach and excellent communication between the clinical team and transfusion laboratory.
- The benefit of routinely transfusing fresh frozen plasma (FFP) in a fixed ratio to red cells ('shock packs') in traumatic haemorrhage is still uncertain but the CRASH-2 trial has proven that early administration of tranexamic acid reduces mortality.
- A restrictive red cell transfusion policy may be appropriate in many patients with acute upper gastrointestinal haemorrhage.

Blood transfusion can be life-saving and is a key component of many modern surgical and medical interventions. However, blood components are expensive, may occasionally have serious adverse effects and supplies are finite. Avoiding unnecessary and inappropriate transfusions is both good for patients and essential to ensure blood supplies meet the increasing demands of an ageing population. Clinical assessment, rather than laboratory test results, should be the most important factor in the decision to transfuse and evidence-based guidelines should be followed where available.

Surgical blood use in the UK has fallen by more than 20% since 2000, at least in part due to the various Better Blood Transfusion initiatives and increasing evidence for the benefits of restrictive transfusion policies. Less than 50% of red cell units are now given to surgical patients. However, audits show that 15–50% of red cell transfusions in a range of surgical procedures are inappropriate and there is still significant variation in the use of blood for the same operations. The fourth edition of the handbook defined good blood management as 'management of the patient at risk of transfusion to minimise the need for allogeneic transfusion, without detriment to the outcome'. Multidisciplinary, evidence-based and patient-centred programmes to achieve this, often called patient blood management

(PBM), are being set up across the UK (http://www.transfusionguidelines.org.uk/Index.
aspx?Publication=NTC&Section=27&pageid=7728) and in other countries, such as
Australia (http://www.nba.gov.au/guidelines/review.html).

# 7.1 Transfusion in surgery

## 7.1.1 Red cell transfusion

Patient blood management should start in primary care at the time of referral for surgery;
working closely with the preoperative assessment clinic at the hospital. It has three
key strands:

**Preoperative optimisation**
- Anaemia (and other relevant health problems) should be identified and treated in a
  timely fashion before surgery.
- Patients at increased risk of bleeding, especially those on anticoagulants or antiplatelet
  drugs, should be recognised.
- The use of blood conservation techniques in appropriate patients should be planned
  in advance.

**Minimising blood loss at surgery**
- Drugs that increase bleeding risk should be withdrawn if safe to do so (discuss with
  prescribing clinician).
- Blood-sparing surgical and anaesthetic techniques should be used.
- Antifibrinolytic drugs, tissue sealants and intraoperative cell salvage procedures should
  be used when appropriate.

**Avoiding unnecessary transfusion after surgery**
- Use restrictive 'transfusion triggers', balancing safety and effectiveness in
  individual patients.
- Minimise blood loss from blood tests.
- Use postoperative red cell salvage and reinfusion where appropriate.
- Prescribe iron and other stimulants to red cell production as needed.

Alternatives to donor blood transfusion and blood conservation techniques are detailed in
Chapter 6. For further useful information about transfusion alternatives see
http://www.nataonline.com/ and http://www.transfusionguidelines.org.uk/.

### 7.1.1.1 Preoperative anaemia

Patients who are anaemic preoperatively (Hb <130 g/L in adult males and Hb <120 g/L in
adult females) are more likely to be transfused and a number of retrospective studies have
shown that preoperative anaemia is an independent risk factor for increased morbidity and
mortality. Ideally, a full blood count is checked at least 6 weeks before planned surgery to
allow time for investigation and treatment and reduce the risk of late cancellation.

Iron deficiency is the most common anaemia revealed by preoperative screening. In men
and post-menopausal women iron deficiency may be an indicator of gastrointestinal
bleeding from peptic disease or cancer and should always be investigated. The speed of
response to oral iron depends on the Hb deficit and the presence of continued blood loss.
At least 3 months of treatment after recovery of Hb is needed to restore body iron stores.
Patients intolerant of full dose oral iron may tolerate a lower dose, albeit with slower
response. Oral iron is ineffective in the early postoperative period because of the inhibitory

effect of inflammation on red cell production. Intravenous iron preparations, which now have a very low incidence of severe allergic reactions, may be used in patients intolerant of oral iron and may also improve the Hb when administered postoperatively (see Chapter 6). Erythropoiesis stimulating agents (ESAs) such as recombinant erythropoietin are not cost-effective in this setting.

## 7.1.1.2  Red cell transfusion in surgery

Clinical factors, as well as the degree of anaemia, must always be considered when making the decision to transfuse. Peripheral blood Hb concentration gives only limited information about the delivery of oxygen to vital organs. Experience of surgical patients who decline red cell transfusion, such as Jehovah's Witnesses, show that otherwise healthy individuals can have successful outcomes down to an Hb concentration as low as 50 g/L (haematocrit approximately 15%) with good supportive care. The 'safe' Hb concentration is likely to be higher in patients with heart or lung disease who are less able to compensate for anaemia.

A number of studies have shown that red cell transfusion is a significant predictor of mortality after cardiac surgery, although its significance in non-cardiac surgery is less clear. Randomised trials of red cell transfusion in haemodynamically stable surgical patients have shown no benefits for liberal transfusion policies in terms of mortality, length of hospital stay or postoperative mobilisation. There is up to a 40% reduction in exposure to donor transfusions when restrictive transfusion thresholds are employed (evidence for the management of more severely ill patients is discussed in section 7.2). Most experts now agree that:

- Transfusion should be considered if Hb below 80 g/L
- If the Hb is below 70 g/L transfusion is usually indicated
- The decision to transfuse should be based on the clinical condition of the patient (higher thresholds may be appropriate in individual cases).

The same 'transfusion triggers' are applicable to patients with asymptomatic cardiovascular disease. Many clinicians recommend using a higher Hb threshold in patients with acute coronary syndromes, but the evidence for this is limited and a recent systematic review actually showed a higher mortality in transfused patients.

The American Association of Blood Banks (AABB) guidelines, published in 2012 (http://www.aabb.org/resources), stress the importance of considering symptoms and expected surgical blood loss as well as the Hb concentration in making the decision to transfuse. The AABB recommendations for red cell transfusion after surgery are as follows:

- Adhere to a restrictive transfusion strategy.
- Consider transfusion if Hb 80 g/L or less.
- Transfuse if symptomatic of anaemia – chest pain, orthostatic hypotension or tachycardia unresponsive to fluid resuscitation, or congestive heart failure.
- The same thresholds can be safely applied to patients with stable cardiovascular disease.

Patients who are not actively bleeding should be transfused with a single unit of red cells and then reassessed before further blood is given.

### 7.1.1.3 Does the age of red cells affect outcome after surgery?

Retrospective observational studies have suggested that transfusing 'older' stored red cells may be associated with higher mortality in patients undergoing cardiac surgery and cardiopulmonary bypass. This is controversial because of confounding factors and conflicting results from other studies. Large randomised trials are in progress to answer this important question. Unless or until there is prospective trial evidence of benefit, specific selection of fresh red cells is not recommended.

## 7.1.2 Bleeding problems in surgical patients

Patients who report abnormal bleeding, especially after dental extractions or surgery, or give a family history of bleeding problems, should be investigated before surgery wherever possible. Patients with known or suspected congenital bleeding disorders should be managed in conjunction with a comprehensive haemophilia care centre (http://www. ukhcdo.org/HaemophiliaCentres/a-c.htm). Most invasive surgical procedures can be carried out safely with a platelet count above $50\times10^9$/L or international normalised ratio (INR) below 2.0.

### 7.1.2.1 Low platelet count

Guidelines for platelet transfusion thresholds in thrombocytopenic surgical patients and patients undergoing invasive procedures are largely based on expert opinion and clinical experience.

Patients who also have impaired blood coagulation (e.g. liver disease, oral anticoagulants) or are on antiplatelet drugs, such as aspirin or clopidogrel, are at higher risk of perioperative bleeding and specialist advice should be sought if major surgery cannot be delayed. The template bleeding time is not a useful screening test for risk of surgical bleeding.

Consensus guidelines commonly used for thrombocytopenic patients requiring surgery are summarised in Table 7.1. When treatment is indicated, a single adult therapeutic dose (ATD) of platelets should be transfused shortly before the procedure and the post-transfusion count checked (10 minutes after transfusion gives a reliable indication).

**Table 7.1 Platelet transfusion thresholds in surgery and invasive procedures**

| Indication | Transfusion threshold or target |
|---|---|
| Most invasive surgery (including post-cardiopulmonary bypass) | $50\times10^9$/L |
| Neurosurgery or posterior eye surgery | $100\times10^9$/L |
| Prevention of bleeding associated with invasive procedures | Lumbar puncture $50\times10^9$/L<br>Central-line insertion $50\times10^9$/L<br>Liver, renal or transbronchial biopsy $50\times10^9$/L<br>Gastrointestinal endoscopy with biopsy $50\times10^9$/L |
| Spinal anaesthesia | $50\times10^9$/L |
| Epidural anaesthesia | $80\times10^9$/L |

Bone marrow aspiration and trephine biopsy can be performed in patients with severe thrombocytopenia without platelet support if adequate local pressure is applied.

## 7.1.2.2  Patients on anticoagulants or antiplatelet drugs

Many older patients scheduled for surgery are on oral anticoagulants or antiplatelet drugs. A decision to temporarily stop the drug or reduce the dose must balance the risk of surgical bleeding against the indication for anticoagulation and be made in collaboration with the prescribing specialist (see 2012 British Committee for Standards in Haematology (BCSH) *Guideline on the Management of Bleeding in Patients on Antithrombotic Agents* (http://www.bcshguidelines.com).

## 7.1.2.3  Warfarin

The current BCSH *Guidelines on Oral Anticoagulation with Warfarin* (http://www. bcshguidelines.com) provide detailed discussion of perioperative management. Minor dental procedures, joint aspiration, cataract surgery and gastrointestinal endoscopic procedures (including biopsy) can be safely carried out on warfarin if the INR is within the therapeutic range. More complex perioperative management should be guided by local protocols and specialist haematological advice. Management options are summarised in Table 7.2.

**Table 7.2 Perioperative management of warfarin anticoagulation (adapted from BCSH *Guidelines on Oral Anticoagulation with Warfarin* – 4th edition, 2011, with permission)**

| | |
|---|---|
| Moderate/high risk of surgical haemorrhage, low risk of thrombosis (e.g. lone atrial fibrillation) | Stop warfarin 5 days preoperatively. Check INR on day before surgery: <br> • If INR <1.5, proceed <br> • INR 1.5 or above, give intravenous vitamin K 1–3 mg <br> Restart maintenance dose of warfarin on evening of surgery if haemostasis secured. |
| Moderate/high risk of surgical haemorrhage, high risk of thrombosis (e.g. mechanical heart valve – especially mitral, venous thromboembolism within last 3 months) | Stop warfarin 5 days preoperatively and give 'bridging therapy' with low molecular weight heparin (LMWH) according to BCSH guideline. <br> Last dose of LMWH 24 hours preoperatively. <br> Restart LMWH when haemostasis secure (at least 48 hours in high bleeding risk surgery). <br> Restart maintenance dose of warfarin when oral intake possible and continue LMWH until INR in therapeutic range. |
| Semi-urgent surgery (within 6–12 hours) | Stop warfarin and give intravenous vitamin K 1–3 mg. <br> Significant correction of INR within 6–8 hours. |
| Emergency surgery or life-threatening bleeding | Stop warfarin. <br> Give 25–50 IU/kg of four factor prothrombin complex concentrate (PCC) and 5 mg intravenous vitamin K. <br> (Fresh frozen plasma produces suboptimal anticoagulation reversal and should only be used if PCC is not available.) |

### 7.1.3 Newer oral anticoagulants

In recent years a number of new oral anticoagulant drugs have been licensed. These include direct oral thrombin inhibitors, such as dabigatran, and direct oral Factor Xa inhibitors, such as rivaroxaban and apixaban. These drugs have no specific antidote. Their half-life is relatively short but can be prolonged in patients with reduced renal function. Wherever possible, treatment should be stopped at least 24 hours before surgery, longer if renal function is impaired (see Summary of Product Characteristics for each drug).

Management of bleeding involves stopping the drug, applying local pressure and administration of antifibrinolytic agents such as tranexamic acid. Fresh frozen plasma (FFP) does not reduce bleeding caused by these drugs. Recombinant activated Factor VII (rFVIIa, NovoSeven™), prothrombin complex concentrate (PCC) and activated PCC (FEIBA™) have been used as a treatment of last resort in uncontrollable bleeding but may increase the risk of thrombosis.

### 7.1.4 Heparins

Unfractionated heparins (UFHs) have a short plasma half-life, but this is increased in the presence of renal dysfunction. They can be administered by intravenous infusion or subcutaneous injection and therapeutic dosing is usually adjusted by comparison of the activated partial thromboplastin time with that of normal pooled plasma (APTT ratio). The anticoagulant effect can be rapidly reversed by injected protamine sulphate (1 mg reverses 80–100 units of UFH, maximum recommended dose 50 mg). Protamine can cause severe allergic reactions and, in most situations, simply discontinuing the UFH is all that is necessary.

Low molecular weight heparins (LMWHs) have a longer half-life, around 3 to 4 hours, which is significantly increased in renal dysfunction. The duration of anticoagulant effect depends on the particular LMWH and is only partially reversible by protamine. LMWHs have a more 'targeted' anticoagulant effect (mainly anti-Xa) than UFH, which may reduce the risk of bleeding, and a lower risk of heparin-induced thrombocytopenia (HIT) and osteopenia. Administration is by subcutaneous injection once or twice daily. They can be prescribed in a fixed or weight-related dose without monitoring in many clinical situations and are convenient for self-administration. Consequently, LMWHs have largely replaced UFH for many routine indications, including thromboprophylaxis for surgery. Perioperative management of patients on heparins is summarised in Table 7.3.

**Table 7.3 Perioperative management of patients on heparins (general guidance only, see Summary of Product Characteristics for specific LMWH)**

| Unfractionated heparins | Stop infusion 6 hours before surgery for full reversal (longer if renal dysfunction) |
|---|---|
| Low molecular weight heparins | Prophylactic dose: stop 12 hours before surgery |
| | Therapeutic dose: stop 24 hours before surgery |

### 7.1.5 Antiplatelet drugs

Aspirin and clopidogrel impair the function of platelets produced during exposure to the drug and the antiplatelet effect takes around 5 days to wear off (varies between individuals). Platelet function analysis or platelet mapping, if available, may give clinically useful information about residual antiplatelet activity. Urgent surgery should not be delayed in patients on these drugs. Many international guidelines recommend clopidogrel is stopped

3 to 5 days before elective surgery because of the risk of perioperative bleeding but the balance of risks and benefits depends on the indication for clopidogrel therapy. Aspirin can be stopped at the time of surgery in cardiac surgery and continued in many surgical procedures except in neurosurgery or operations on the inner eye.

Non-steroidal anti-inflammatory drugs (NSAIDs) produce reversible platelet dysfunction and have a short duration of action. Most guidelines suggest they are stopped at least 2 days before surgery associated with significant bleeding risk. Studies in elective orthopaedic surgery (mainly hip replacement) show increased blood loss and transfusion requirements in those who continue NSAID therapy to the time of surgery. The optimum time to discontinue NSAIDs prior to orthopaedic surgery is uncertain. Some guidelines have suggested a 2-week interval but acknowledge the evidence base for this is weak.

Inhibitors of platelet surface receptors GPIIb/IIIa may be used in patients with acute coronary syndromes. Abciximab inhibits platelet function for 12 to 24 hours after administration whereas eptifibatide and tirofibam have a short half-life of 1.5 to 2.5 hours. Invasive surgery should be delayed for 12–24 hours if possible. The drug effect is partially reversible by platelet transfusion.

## 7.1.6 Systemic fibrinolytic agents

'Clot-busting' drugs may be used in acute myocardial infarction, acute ischaemic stroke or massive pulmonary embolism. Streptokinase has a variable half-life, depending on the presence of anti-streptococcal antibodies, but can reduce fibrinogen and anti-plasmin levels for several days. With recombinant tissue plasminogen activator (e.g. alteplase) fibrinogen levels are only modestly reduced, usually returning to normal within 24 hours. Treatment for haemorrhage due to these drugs, or preparation for emergency surgery, may include antifibrinolytic agents (tranexamic acid or aprotinin – see Chapter 6), transfusion of FFP and cryoprecipitate or fibrinogen concentrate (not licensed for this indication) if the plasma fibrinogen is <1 g/L.

## 7.1.7 Cardiopulmonary bypass

Cardiopulmonary bypass (CPB) causes thrombocytopenia and platelet dysfunction that can increase the risk of haemorrhage. Prophylactic transfusion of platelets (or other blood components) is not beneficial but antifibrinolytic agents, such as aprotinin and tranexamic acid, may reduce blood loss. Thromboelastography (TEG) or rotational thromboelastometry (ROTEM), usually performed in the operating room, may be helpful in guiding blood component therapy when excess bleeding occurs.

## 7.1.8 Liver transplantation

Transfusion requirements for liver transplantation have fallen significantly, but substantial, complex blood component support may still be necessary. Problems include preoperative coagulopathy due to liver disease, difficult surgery with the risk of high blood losses and intraoperative coagulopathy and hyperfibrinolysis before the transplanted liver starts to function. Intraoperative red cell salvage is effective in reducing donor blood transfusion and TEG is often used to direct blood component transfusion with FFP and platelets. Antifibrinolytic therapy with tranexamic acid or aprotinin may be beneficial in individual cases.

# 7.2    Transfusion in critically ill patients

Patients admitted to critical care units often receive blood transfusions but there is increasing evidence of potential harm as well as benefit. Clinical audits show that transfusions of platelets and FFP are often given for indications outside consensus guidelines.

## 7.2.1    Red cell transfusion in critical care

More than half of all patients admitted to critical care are anaemic and 30% of these have an initial Hb of <90 g/L. Anaemia early after admission is mainly caused by haemorrhage, haemodilution and frequent blood sampling. Later, reduced red cell production due to inflammation becomes an important factor and 80% of patients have an Hb of <90 g/L after 7 days. Around 80% of these transfusions are given to correct a low Hb rather than treat active bleeding. Blood losses from phlebotomy can be reduced by the use of blood conservation sampling devices and paediatric blood sample tubes.

Transfusion management has been strongly influenced by the 1999 Transfusion Requirements In Critical Care (TRICC) study (http://www.ncbi.nlm.nih.gov/pubmed/9971864) which randomised patients to an Hb 'transfusion trigger' of 100 g/L (liberal) or 70 g/L (restrictive). There was a trend to lower mortality in patients randomised to a restrictive policy (30% of whom received no transfusions). This was statistically significant in younger patients (<55 years) and those less severely ill. A restrictive transfusion policy was associated with lower rates of new organ failures and acute respiratory distress syndrome. Randomised trials in paediatric critical care, cardiac surgery, elderly patients undergoing 'high-risk' hip surgery and gastrointestinal haemorrhage have shown no advantages for a liberal transfusion policy.

A higher transfusion trigger may be beneficial in patients with ischaemic stroke, traumatic brain injury with cerebral ischaemia, acute coronary syndrome (ACS) or in the early stages of severe sepsis. There is no current evidence to support the use of 'fresh' rather than stored red cells in critically ill patients or the routine use of erythropoiesis stimulating agents.

The evidence base is reviewed in the 2012 BCSH *Guidelines on the Management of Anaemia and Red Cell Transfusion in Adult Critically Ill Patients* (http://www.bcshguidelines.com) and the guideline recommendations are summarised in Figure 7.1.

## 7.2.2    Platelet transfusion in critical care

Moderate thrombocytopenia (>50×10$^9$/L) is common in critical care patients, often associated with sepsis or disseminated intravascular coagulation (DIC). 'Prophylactic' platelet transfusion in non-bleeding patients is not indicated, although this is the most common reason for transfusion identified in clinical audits (followed by 'cover' for invasive procedures). There are no high-quality randomised controlled trials to guide clinical practice and a BCSH guideline is currently in development.

The risk of bleeding in thrombocytopenic patients may be reduced by the avoidance or withdrawal of antiplatelet agents (e.g. aspirin, clopidogrel or non-steroidal anti-inflammatory drugs) and the use of antifibrinolytics such as tranexamic acid. Guidelines based on observational studies and expert opinion are summarised in Table 7.4.

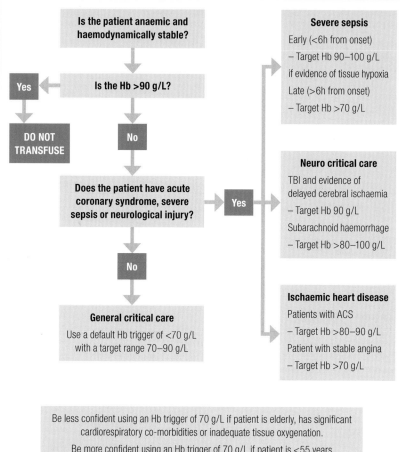

**Figure 7.1 Guidelines for red cell transfusion in critical care (adapted by courtesy of British Committee for Standards in Haematology)**

Is the patient anaemic and haemodynamically stable?

Is the Hb >90 g/L?

Yes

DO NOT TRANSFUSE

No

Does the patient have acute coronary syndrome, severe sepsis or neurological injury?

Yes

No

**General critical care**
Use a default Hb trigger of <70 g/L with a target range 70–90 g/L

**Severe sepsis**
Early (<6h from onset)
– Target Hb 90–100 g/L
if evidence of tissue hypoxia
Late (>6h from onset)
– Target Hb >70 g/L

**Neuro critical care**
TBI and evidence of delayed cerebral ischaemia
– Target Hb 90 g/L
Subarachnoid haemorrhage
– Target Hb >80–100 g/L

**Ischaemic heart disease**
Patients with ACS
– Target Hb >80–90 g/L
Patient with stable angina
– Target Hb >70 g/L

Be less confident using an Hb trigger of 70 g/L if patient is elderly, has significant cardiorespiratory co-morbidities or inadequate tissue oxygenation.

Be more confident using an Hb trigger of 70 g/L if patient is <55 years and/or the severity of illness is relatively low.

ACS – acute coronary syndrome
TBI – traumatic brain injury

**Table 7.4 Suggested indications for platelet transfusion in adult critical care**

| Indication | Transfusion threshold or target |
|---|---|
| Non-bleeding patients without severe sepsis or haemostatic abnormalities | Not indicated |
| Prophylaxis in non-bleeding patients with severe sepsis or haemostatic abnormalities | Threshold $20\times10^9$/L |
| DIC with bleeding | Maintain $>50\times10^9$/L |
| Platelet dysfunction with non-surgically correctable bleeding (e.g. post-cardiopulmonary bypass or potent antiplatelet drugs) | May bleed despite a normal platelet count. Transfusion of one adult therapeutic dose and repeat according to clinical response |
| Major haemorrhage and massive transfusion | Maintain $>75\times10^9$/L ($>100\times10^9$/L if multiple trauma or trauma to the central nervous system or inner eye) |

## 7.2.3   Plasma component transfusion in critical care

A study of UK critical care units in 2011 showed that 13% of patients received transfusions of FFP. Around 40% of these transfusions were given to non-bleeding patients with normal or only mildly deranged clotting tests and many doses were subtherapeutic. Cryoprecipitate is used as a concentrated source of fibrinogen (fibrinogen concentrate is not yet licensed in the UK for this use). More research is needed to define best practice but the following pragmatic guidelines are suggested:

**Fresh frozen plasma**
■ Indicated for the treatment of bleeding in patients with deranged coagulation due to deficiency of multiple clotting factors (e.g. DIC).
■ Minimum dose 12–15 mL/kg (equivalent to four units in an average adult).
■ Not indicated for prophylaxis in non-bleeding patients with abnormal clotting tests.
■ Not indicated for the immediate reversal of warfarin (PCC should be used).
■ In liver disease, there is no benefit to FFP transfusions in patients with an INR less than 1.7.

**Cryoprecipitate**
■ Adult dose is two pooled units (ten donor units – approximately 3 g fibrinogen).
■ Indications include:
  • acute DIC with bleeding and fibrinogen <1.5 g/L
  • severe liver disease with bleeding
  • prophylaxis for surgery when fibrinogen <1.5 g/L
  • hypofibrinogenaemia associated with massive transfusion (maintain >1.5 g/L).

# 7.3   Transfusion management of major haemorrhage

Major haemorrhage is variously defined as:

■ Loss of more than one blood volume within 24 hours (around 70 mL/kg, >5 litres in a 70 kg adult)

- 50% of total blood volume lost in less than 3 hours
- Bleeding in excess of 150 mL/minute.

A pragmatic clinically based definition is bleeding which leads to a systolic blood pressure of less than 90 mm Hg or a heart rate of more than 110 beats per minute.

Early recognition and intervention is essential for survival. The immediate priorities are to control bleeding (surgery and interventional radiology) and maintain vital organ perfusion by transfusing blood and other fluids through a wide-bore intravenous catheter. Recent research has focused on major traumatic haemorrhage, influenced by the increased survival of military casualties using 'damage control resuscitation' and early transfusion of fresh plasma and red cells (see below).

Successful management of major haemorrhage requires a protocol-driven multidisciplinary team approach with involvement of medical, anaesthetic and surgical staff of sufficient seniority and experience, underpinned by clear lines of communication between clinicians and the transfusion laboratory. Useful information on the development of major haemorrhage protocols can be found on the UK Blood Transfusion and Tissue Transplantation Services website (http://www.transfusionguidelines.org.uk/Index.aspx?pageid=7675&publication=RTC) and the Association of Anaesthetists' guideline on management of massive haemorrhage (http://www.aagbi.org/sites/default/files/massive_haemorrhage_2010_0.pdf).

Major haemorrhage protocols should identify the key roles of team leader (often the most senior doctor directing resuscitation of the patient) and coordinator responsible for communicating with laboratories and other support services to prevent time-wasting and often confusing duplicate calls. In an emergency situation it is essential to ensure correct transfusion identification procedures for patients, samples and blood components are performed (see Chapter 4) and an accurate record is kept of all blood components transfused. Training of clinical and laboratory staff and regular 'fire drills' to test the protocol and ensure the rapid delivery of all blood components are essential.

An example of a practical algorithm for the transfusion management of major haemorrhage is given in Figure 7.2.

## 7.3.1 Red cell transfusion in major haemorrhage

Red cell transfusion is usually necessary if 30–40% blood volume is lost, and rapid loss of >40% is immediately life threatening. Peripheral blood haematocrit and Hb concentration may be misleading early after major acute blood loss and the initial diagnosis of major haemorrhage requiring transfusion should be based on clinical criteria and observations (see Figure 7.2).

For immediate transfusion, group O red cells should be issued after samples are taken for blood grouping and crossmatching. Females less than 50 years of age should receive RhD negative red cells to avoid sensitisation. The use of Kell negative red cells is also desirable in this group. Group O red cells must continue to be issued if patient or sample identification is incomplete or until the ABO group is confirmed on a second sample according to local policy (see Chapter 2).

ABO-group-specific red cells can usually be issued within 10 minutes of a sample arriving in the laboratory. Fully crossmatched blood is available in 30 to 40 minutes after a sample is received in the laboratory. Once the volume of blood transfused in any 24 hour period is equivalent to the patient's own blood volume (8–10 units for adults and 80–100 mL/kg in children), ABO and D compatible blood can be issued without the need for a serological crossmatch.

**Figure 7.2 Algorithm for the management of major haemorrhage (adapted from the BCSH *Practical Guideline for the Management of Those With, or At Risk of Major Haemorrhage* (2013) with permission)**

Recognise blood loss and trigger major blood loss protocol

⬇

Take baseline blood samples before transfusion for:
- Full blood count, group and save, clotting screen including Clauss fibrinogen
- Near-patient haemostasis testing if available

⬇

If trauma and <3h from injury, give tranexamic acid 1 g bolus over 10 minutes followed by IV infusion of 1 g over 8h (consider tranexamic acid 1 g bolus in non-traumatic)

⬇

Team leader to coordinate management and nominate a member of team to liaise with transfusion laboratory
- State patient unique identifier and location when requesting components
- To limit use of Group O NEG: until patient group known, use O NEG units in females and consider O POS in males
- Use group-specific blood as soon as available
- Request agreed ratio of blood components (e.g. 6 units RBS and 4 units FFP). Send porter to lab to collect urgently

⬇

If bleeding continues

⬇

**Until lab results are available:**
- Give further FFP 1L (4 units) per 6 units red cells
- Consider cryoprecipitate (2 pools)
- Consider platelets (1 adult therapeutic dose (ATD))

**If lab results are available:**

| IF | GIVE |
|---|---|
| Falling Hb | Red cells |
| PT ratio >1.5 | FFP 15–20 mL/kg |
| Fibrinogen <1.5 g/L | Cryoprecipitate (2 pools) |
| Platelets <75×10$^9$/L | Platelets 1 ATD |

⬇

Continue cycle of clinical and laboratory monitoring and administration of 'goal-directed' blood component therapy until bleeding stops

The use of intraoperative cell salvage devices reduces the need for donor red cells in appropriate cases. When bleeding is controlled and the patient enters the critical care unit, a restrictive red cell transfusion policy is probably appropriate.

## 7.3.2 Coagulation and major haemorrhage

The transfusion of large volumes of red cells and other intravenous fluids that contain no coagulation factors or platelets causes dilutional coagulopathy. Major traumatic haemorrhage is often associated with activation of the coagulation and fibrinolytic systems ('acute traumatic coagulopathy'). Plasma fibrinogen predictably falls to sub-haemostatic levels (<1.5 g/L) after 1 to 1.5 blood volume replacement (earlier in the presence of coagulopathy and hyperfibrinolysis). Coagulation is also impaired by hypothermia, acidosis and reduced ionised calcium ($Ca^{2+}$) concentration (which can be measured on many blood gas analysers). Ionised hypocalcaemia may be caused by rapid transfusion of blood components containing citrate anticoagulant, although this is uncommon in the presence of normal liver function.

Traditional 'massive transfusion' guidelines use laboratory tests such as prothrombin time (PT) and activated partial thromboplastin time (APTT) to guide blood component replacement. The usefulness of these tests is reduced by the significant delay between sampling and returning results to the clinical team. If a PT can be made available with a rapid turnaround time that allows it to reflect the clinical situation it can be used to aid decisions regarding FFP infusion. The Clauss fibrinogen assay should be used in preference to a fibrinogen estimated from the optical change in the PT (PT-derived fibrinogen) that can be misleading in this setting.

Point of care testing (POCT) has an increasing role in providing 'real time' laboratory data to guide blood component replacement. It is essential to ensure appropriate calibration and quality assurance of POCT devices. Assays of clot formation, clot strength and lysis, such as thromboelastography (TEG) or rotational thromboelastometry (ROTEM), have been used for many years to inform plasma and platelet transfusion in liver transplantation and cardiac surgery. Their value in the management of major haemorrhage is uncertain and is the subject of current research.

FFP should be transfused in doses of 12–15 mL/kg (at least four units in the average adult) to maintain the PT ratio (compared to 'normal pooled plasma') less than 1.5. Fibrinogen levels should be maintained above 1.5 g/L (Table 7.5).

**Table 7.5  Options for fibrinogen replacement**

| Source of fibrinogen | Dose to raise fibrinogen by about 1 g/L in adult patient |
| --- | --- |
| Fresh frozen plasma (FFP) | 4 units (about 15 mL/kg) |
| Cryoprecipitate | 2 five-unit pools |
| Fibrinogen concentrate[a] | 3 to 4 g |

[a] Currently not licensed in the UK for acquired hypofibrinogenaemia

The early transfusion of FFP in a fixed ratio to red cells ('shock packs') in traumatic haemorrhage, to reverse coagulopathy and reduce bleeding, has been extrapolated from military to civilian practice but the true value of this approach is uncertain. Retrospective studies are confounded by 'survivorship bias' (the most severely injured patients do not survive long enough to be transfused) and the non-military trauma population is older and less fit. Transfusion policy is just one component of an integrated, multidisciplinary response to major trauma. Large-volume FFP transfusion carries increased risks of circulatory overload (TACO), allergic reactions and transfusion-related acute lung injury (TRALI), and further clinical research is required to clarify its role.

Once haemostasis is secured, prophylactic anticoagulation with low molecular weight heparin should be considered because of the risk of thromboembolic complications.

### 7.3.3 Platelets and major haemorrhage

The platelet count usually remains above $50\times10^9$/L (the generally accepted haemostatic level) until 1.5 to 2.5 blood volumes have been replaced. Many hospitals do not store platelets on site and the time for transfer from the blood centre must be factored into local protocols. Therefore, an adult therapeutic dose should be requested when the count falls to $75\times10^9$/L.

### 7.3.4 Pharmacological treatments in major haemorrhage

The CRASH-2 trial published in 2010 clearly showed that early administration of the antifibrinolytic drug tranexamic acid improves the survival of patients with major traumatic haemorrhage or at risk of significant bleeding after trauma (Chapter 6). Tranexamic acid should be given as soon as possible after the injury in a dose of 1 g over 10 minutes followed by a maintenance infusion of 1 g over 8 hours. Evidence is emerging of the value of tranexamic acid in other forms of major haemorrhage, including obstetric and surgical haemorrhage. Given its good safety profile, ease of administration and low cost, tranexamic acid should be considered as a component of most major haemorrhage protocols.

Recombinant activated Factor VII (rFVIIa, NovoSeven™) is widely used off-label as a 'last ditch' therapy for patients with major haemorrhage (see Chapter 6). Systematic reviews and registry studies show no good evidence of improved survival, and life-threatening arterial and venous thromboembolic complications may occur, particularly in older patients with vascular disease. Several national guidelines no longer recommend its use outside research studies. Local protocols that include rFVIIa should require advice and authorisation from a haematologist or coagulation specialist and ensure that adverse effects are monitored and recorded.

### 7.3.5 Acute upper gastrointestinal bleeding

Acute upper gastrointestinal bleeding (AUGIB) is common and has a case fatality of around 10%. Some 35% of bleeds are caused by peptic ulcer disease but the most severe haemorrhage and highest mortality is seen in the 10% of cases presenting with bleeding from oesophageal or gastric varices. Treatment of AUGIB consumes around 14% of red cell units issued in the UK. Evidence-based guidelines for management were published in 2012 by the National Institute for Health and Care Evidence (NICE – http://www.nice.org.uk/nicemedia/live/13762/59549/59549.pdf).

Initial resuscitation of patients with massive gastrointestinal haemorrhage should include transfusion of red cells, platelets and clotting factors according to the local major haemorrhage protocol. In patients who are actively bleeding, the platelet count should be maintained $>50\times10^9$/L, PT ratio >1.5 and fibrinogen >1.5 g/L. PCC and intravenous vitamin K should be used if immediate warfarin reversal is needed. It may be logical to administer PCC, which contains the liver-derived clotting Factors II, VII, IX and X, in bleeding patients with liver failure, but its use in this situation is off-label.

Once the patient is haemodynamically stable, and in patients with less severe initial haemorrhage, over-transfusion may increase the risk of recurrent bleeding (probably by increasing portal venous pressure) and increase mortality. In a recent large randomised trial in patients with severe (but not massive) upper gastrointestinal haemorrhage in Spain (Villanueva *et al.*, 2013), mortality and re-bleeding was lower in patients randomised to a restrictive rather than a liberal red cell transfusion policy (transfusion trigger 70 or 90 g/L). There were more adverse events (reactions and circulatory overload) in the liberal group. Of note, the trial excluded patients with a history of ischaemic heart disease, stroke or vascular disease and the results may not be generalisable, especially to older patients. Transfusion strategy in AUGIB is the subject of a current UK multicentre randomised trial (TRIGGER – http://www.nhsbt.nhs.uk/trigger) which is recruiting unselected cases in six hospitals.

## 7.3.6    Major obstetric haemorrhage

See section 9.4.

## 7.3.7    Audit of the management of major haemorrhage

Audit is important to assess adverse events, timeliness of blood component support, patient outcome and component wastage. There should be multidisciplinary review of cases that trigger the major blood loss protocol to ensure it is being applied appropriately and effectively. Serious adverse reactions (SAR), serious adverse events (SAE) or incidents of patient harm due to delay should be reported to the Serious Hazards of Transfusion (SHOT) scheme (http://www.shotuk.org) (SAE and SAR must also be reported to the Medicines and Healthcare Products Regulatory Agency, MHRA).

# 8

# EFFECTIVE TRANSFUSION
# IN MEDICAL PATIENTS

# Essentials

- Inappropriate blood transfusions in medical patients are common and may cause harm.
- Blood transfusion should not be performed where there are appropriate alternatives such as haematinic replacement (in iron deficiency) or erythropoiesis stimulating agents (in chronic kidney disease).
- There is no universal transfusion trigger – the decision to transfuse should be based on clinical assessment of the patient, supported by the results of laboratory tests and informed by evidence-based guidelines.
- Haemodynamically stable haemato-oncology patients who are anaemic after intensive chemotherapy rarely need transfusion if the Hb is >80 g/L.
- Treatment of patients dependent on long-term transfusion (e.g. myelodysplasia) should aim to minimise symptoms of anaemia and improve health-related quality of life rather than achieve an arbitrary Hb concentration.
- Prophylactic platelet transfusions should be given to patients receiving intensive chemotherapy, with a transfusion trigger of $10\times10^9$/L.
- Platelet prophylaxis is not required for bone marrow aspiration or trephine biopsy and a level of $50\times10^9$/L is safe for other invasive procedures.
- Component selection errors for patients who have changed blood group after allogeneic haemopoietic stem cell transplantation are common and often stem from poor communication between clinical and laboratory teams.
- Transfusion in patients with haemoglobinopathies (thalassaemia and sickle cell disease) is complex and changing. It should be directed by specialist teams in line with national guidelines and research evidence.
- Transfusion reactions in patients with sickle cell disease may be misinterpreted as sickle cell crises and treated incorrectly.

More than 50% of red cells in the UK are transfused for non-surgical indications. The recipients are often elderly and have an increased risk of transfusion complications such as transfusion-associated circulatory overload (TACO). Although overall red cell demand has fallen in the UK in the last decade, largely because of a reduction in surgical transfusions, there has been a continuing rise in requests for platelets and fresh frozen plasma (FFP).

The decision to transfuse, and how much, should be based on clinical assessment and clearly defined objectives, such as reduction in fatigue, not on the Hb level alone. Evidence-based guidelines improve the balance between efficacy and safety as well as improving the economy of blood use. Alternatives to donor blood should be used where appropriate. The introduction of computerised ordering systems for blood components offers the opportunity to link requests to 'real time' laboratory data and provide on-screen decision support to the prescriber based on best evidence for the clinical indication. Inappropriate transfusions have been significantly reduced by the introduction of such systems in certain US hospitals (Murphy *et al.*, 2013).

The biggest medical users of blood are haematology, oncology, gastrointestinal medicine (including liver disease) and renal medicine (*National Comparative Audit of Blood Transfusion – 2011 Audit of Use of Blood in Adult Medical Patients – Part 1* http://hospital. blood.co.uk/library/pdf/Medical_Use_Audit_Part_1_Report.pdf). The median age of transfused patients in this audit was 73 years and nearly half were transfused outside current national guidelines. It was found that 20% of patients were transfused despite having a treatable cause for anaemia, such as iron deficiency; 29% were transfused at an Hb concentration above the predefined 'trigger'; and patients were often transfused up to a higher than necessary Hb concentration (especially patients of low body weight).

# 8.1    Haematinic deficiencies

## 8.1.1    Iron deficiency anaemia

The diagnosis, investigation and management of iron deficiency anaemia are discussed in more detail in Chapter 7. The underlying cause should be identified and treated if possible. In most cases, iron deficiency anaemia can be treated with oral iron. Safe intravenous iron preparations (see Chapter 6) are now available for patients who do not tolerate oral iron. In patients without acute blood loss, transfusion should only be considered if an immediate increase in Hb concentration is essential on clinical grounds – symptoms of severe anaemia such as chest pain or congestive heart failure. The minimum number of red cell units should be transfused with careful monitoring to 'buy time' for a response to iron therapy. One-unit transfusions are perfectly acceptable in this situation, especially for small, elderly patients at risk of TACO.

## 8.1.2    Vitamin B12 or folate deficiency

Deficiency of vitamin B12 or folate produces megaloblastic changes in bone marrow cells and anaemia with large ('macrocytic') red cells in the peripheral blood. Vitamin B12 deficiency is most often due to autoimmune pernicious anaemia with failure to absorb B12 in the terminal ileum. Folate deficiency usually results from dietary deficiency, consumption by increased red cell production (such as pregnancy or haemolytic anaemia) or malabsorption in coeliac disease. Patients may present with very low Hb concentrations. Treatment is with intramuscular B12 injections or oral folic acid. Severe megaloblastic anaemia causes impaired cardiac muscle function and red cell transfusion should be avoided wherever possible because of the risk of causing potentially fatal circulatory overload. Patients with severe symptomatic anaemia can often be treated with bed rest and high-concentration oxygen while a response to B12 or folate occurs (the Hb concentration starts to rise in 3 or 4 days). If red cell transfusion is essential, single units of red cells should be transfused over 4 hours with close monitoring and diuretic cover. Red cell exchange transfusion may also be considered.

# 8.2    Anaemia of chronic disease (ACD)

This is the most common chronic anaemia encountered in hospital practice. ACD is caused by high levels of inflammatory cytokines and is seen in patients with inflammatory, infectious or malignant diseases as well as conditions such as diabetes and congestive heart failure. There is reduced production of red cells in the bone marrow, impaired utilisation of iron by red cell precursors and a 'blunted' response to erythropoietin (Epo). The anaemia is often mild and fluctuates with disease activity or response to treatment of the underlying medical condition. If patients are symptomatic from anaemia or Hb levels need to be improved before surgery (e.g. joint replacement in patients with rheumatoid arthritis), treatment with intravenous iron or an erythropoiesis stimulating agent (ESA) may be beneficial. ACD in patients with active rheumatoid arthritis or inflammatory bowel disease may be improved by treatment with monoclonal antibodies, such as anti-TNF, that reduce the inflammatory response.

## 8.3   Anaemia in cancer patients

Anaemia is common in patients with cancer and is a major cause of debilitating fatigue and impaired health-related quality of life (HRQoL). Causes include infiltration of bone marrow by malignant cells, suppression of red cell production by inflammatory cytokines (as in ACD), or cytotoxic chemotherapy, nutritional deficiencies, renal damage and bleeding.

Treatment of anaemia in cancer patients centres on red cell transfusions or ESAs. The decision to treat should be based on symptoms such as fatigue, breathlessness and impaired quality of life rather than a specific Hb concentration, and relief of symptoms is the target of therapy. Radiotherapy may be less effective in the presence of anaemia (hypoxic cancer cells are less sensitive to radiation) but the benefit of red cell transfusion to reduce mild anaemia in this setting is controversial.

Treatment with ESA (e.g. rHuEpo or darbopoietin) can modestly reduce blood transfusion exposure and improve HRQoL in selected cancer patients, especially in those treated with nephrotoxic platinum compounds. The maximum improvement in fatigue and HRQoL occurs between Hb 110 and 120 g/L. However, there is increasing evidence that ESAs can promote the growth of a range of non-haematological tumours. They may also increase the already raised risk of venous and arterial thromboembolism in cancer patients. ESAs should only be used where clinical trials have shown unequivocal benefits and in accordance with consensus guidelines such as those of the American Society of Clinical Oncology (http://www.asco.org/institute-quality/asco-ash-clinical-practice-guideline-update-use-epoetin-and-darbepoetin-adult).

## 8.4   Anaemia and renal disease

Worsening anaemia is a feature of chronic kidney disease (CKD) once the glomerular filtration rate falls below 60 mL/minute. It causes fatigue and impaired quality of life and may increase damage to the heart.

The major cause of renal anaemia is deficiency of erythropoietin (Epo), which is produced in the kidneys. Contributing factors include shortened red cell lifespan, inflammation, impaired release of iron from body stores and blood loss during haemodialysis. Most patients with severe CKD and symptomatic anaemia respond well to treatment with ESAs such as rHuEpo (see Chapter 6) and these can eliminate the need for blood transfusion. Parenteral iron supplements are often required to produce a full response. Because of the risk of hypertension and thrombotic complications with higher haematocrit levels, patients must be carefully monitored and the ESA dose adjusted to obtain maximum improvement in quality of life while avoiding Hb levels above 120 g/L. Successful renal transplantation corrects the anaemia of CKD.

## 8.5   Transfusion and organ transplantation

### 8.5.1   Renal transplantation

It is important to avoid unnecessary blood transfusions in potential renal transplant recipients as exposure to multiple blood donations may cause alloimmunisation to human leucocyte antigen (HLA) class I antigens on white blood cells. HLA antibodies can react with the transplanted kidney leading to higher rates of acute rejection and poorer long-term graft survival. The risk of alloimmunisation has reduced since the introduction of universal leucodepletion of blood components and the use of ESA in CKD.

ABO-incompatible renal transplants have traditionally been avoided because of a high incidence of failure due to hyperacute graft rejection. To increase the pool of potential donors, pre-transplant protocols that combine plasma exchange with immunosuppressive therapy and immunoadsorption columns to remove ABO antibodies from the patient's blood are proving increasingly successful.

Irradiated cellular blood components are currently recommended for solid organ transplant patients who have received alemtuzumab (anti-CD52) as immunosuppressive therapy (see section 8.7).

### 8.5.2 Haemolysis after ABO-incompatible solid organ transplantation

Transplanted organs may contain donor B-lymphocytes capable of producing ABO antibodies. Transplantation of the liver from a blood group O donor to a patient of other ABO groups, especially group A, can cause immune haemolysis of the recipient's red cells 7 to 10 days post-transplant ('passenger lymphocyte syndrome'). This is usually mild and resolves within 4 weeks but may require treatment with steroids or red cell transfusion (with group O blood). Passenger lymphocyte syndrome can complicate other solid organ transplants, depending on the lymphoid cell content of the transplanted organ. It is rare with renal transplants but much more common in heart–lung and small bowel transplants.

# 8.6    Haemoglobinopathies

Haemoglobin (Hb) molecules consist of four haem (iron-containing) complexes and four globin chains (two $\alpha$ and two non-$\alpha$ chains – Table 8.1). The haem component carries oxygen and the globin chains contribute to the stability and oxygen affinity of the Hb molecule.

Table 8.1  Normal adult haemoglobins

| Haemoglobin | Globin chains | % of total Hb in adult |
|---|---|---|
| A | $2\alpha/2\beta$ | >95% |
| A2 | $2\alpha/2\delta$ | <3.5% |
| F | $2\alpha/2\gamma$ | <1% |

Haemoglobinopathies are inherited disorders, usually autosomal recessive. Carriers (heterozygotes), with just one abnormal gene, are usually asymptomatic, whereas people who inherit an abnormal gene from both parents (homozygotes) express the disease. In most parts of the UK there is a programme of antenatal and neonatal screening for the most serious variants. Haemoglobinopathies fall into two main categories:

■ **Thalassaemias** Reduced or absent production of normal $\alpha$ or $\beta$-globin chains, leading to reduced levels of HbA, the main adult Hb. They are very diverse disorders at the genetic and clinical levels.

■ **Abnormal haemoglobins** A new Hb variant results from mutations in the genes for α or β globin chains that alter the stability or other functions of the Hb molecule (e.g. sickle Hb (HbS)).

## 8.6.1    β-thalassaemia major

By definition, β-thalassaemia major patients are transfusion dependent. Caused by impaired production of normal β-globin chains, this condition is most common in people whose ancestors originate from the Mediterranean, Middle East, South or Southeast Asia or the Far East. There are more than 1000 patients with this condition in the UK. Life-threatening anaemia develops in the first year of life as levels of fetal Hb (HbF) decline and adult HbA cannot be produced. Most patients are transfusion dependent for life, although some may be cured by haemopoietic stem cell transplantation in childhood. Undertreated anaemia leads to enlargement of the spleen, expansion of the bone marrow and skeletal abnormalities. The UK Thalassaemia Society has produced *Standards for the Clinical Care of Children and Adults with Thalassaemia in the UK* (http://www.hbpinfo.com/ukts-standards-2008.pdf) that includes recommendations on transfusion support.

Transfusions are usually given every 3 to 4 weeks to keep the pre-transfusion Hb concentration above 95–105 g/L (average Hb 120 g/L). This allows normal growth and development and prevents skeletal deformity due to bone marrow expansion. However, each transfused red cell unit contains up to 250 mg of iron and iron chelation therapy must be given from the age of 2 to 3 years to prevent organ damage, and eventual death, from iron deposition in the heart, liver, pancreas and endocrine glands. Chelation usually starts when the ferritin level exceeds 1000 ng/mL (after around ten transfusions). Options for reducing iron overload include subcutaneous desferrioxamine infusions on 5 to 7 nights a week and/or the newer oral chelating agents. The practice of infusing desferrioxamine only at the time of transfusion is of little benefit and it must not be added to the red cell transfusion pack. Before starting transfusion children should be given hepatitis B immunisation.

## 8.6.2    Red cell alloimmunisation in thalassaemia

Up to 30% of patients on long-term transfusion support develop blood group antibodies (alloimmunisation), most commonly to Rh and Kell antigens. There may be progressive difficulty in providing compatible blood. If possible, 'extended phenotyping' is carried out before the first transfusion and red cells matched for Rh (D, C, c, E, e) and K antigens should be routinely selected. This policy appears to reduce the risk of developing alloantibodies to other blood group systems. Donor exposure can be reduced by selecting larger volume red cell units from the blood bank, preferably less than 14 days old, and the transfusion of 'double red cell donations' taken from a single donor by apheresis.

## 8.6.3    Sickle cell disease

Sickle cell disease (SCD) is characterised by:

■ Vaso-occlusive episodes causing recurrent acute painful sickle cell crises and syndromes such as stroke or acute chest syndrome
■ Chronic haemolytic anaemia (Hb commonly 60 to 80 g/L in HbS/S)
■ Splenic atrophy and hyposplenism (due to splenic infarction) with increased susceptibility to sudden overwhelming infection by encapsulated bacteria such as *Streptococcus pneumoniae* and *Streptococcus meningitidis*
■ Chronic organ damage, such as chronic kidney disease and joint damage from avascular necrosis, caused by recurrent sickling episodes.

8 Effective transfusion

Patients with SCD are predominantly of Black African descent, although the sickle (HbS) gene also occurs in populations of Mediterranean, Arab and South Asian origin. Most patients with severe SCD are homozygous for the HbS gene (HbS/S) but combinations can occur with other haemoglobinopathies to produce sickling syndromes of variable severity such as sickle-β-thalassaemia, HbS/C or HbS/E. There are more than 12500 patients with SCD in the UK.

## 8.6.4 Red cell transfusion in sickle cell disease

There are UK standards and guidelines for the clinical care of sickle cell disease in children (http://sct.screening.nhs.uk/cms.php?folder=2493) and adults (http://www.sicklecellsociety. org/app/webroot/files/files/CareBook.pdf) that include recommendations for transfusion.

Red cell transfusion in SCD is used in the treatment of acute sickle cell crises or to prevent certain long-term complications by reducing the proportion of HbS cells in the circulation (Tables 8.2 and 8.3). However, increasing the haematocrit above 30% increases the risk of hyperviscosity and vaso-occlusive events. Red cell exchange transfusion, automated or manual, can produce a significant reduction in HbS (target usually <30%) without the risk of hyperviscosity but venous access can be problematic in patients requiring regular or recurrent treatment. Indications for transfusion are developing quickly and the decision to transfuse should always be made in collaboration with the expert team at a comprehensive haemoglobinopathy centre.

Large, multicentre trials are exploring the benefits/risks of prophylactic transfusion in surgery. At present, exchange transfusion is usually only carried out in patients with severe SCD undergoing major surgical procedures. For 'medium-risk' surgery, 'top-up' transfusion (to 80–100 g/L) appears to be as effective as exchange transfusion and may be safer. Current evidence does not support the routine use of transfusion to prevent fetal complications in pregnancy but each patient requires careful multidisciplinary review. Following evidence from randomised controlled trials that prophylactic hypertransfusion (target HbS <25%, Hb 100–145 g/L) reduces the risk of stroke in children with abnormal flow in intracranial blood vessels, demonstrated by transcranial Doppler (TCD) screening, the numbers of SCD patients on long-term or lifelong transfusion regimens will increase significantly.

Table 8.2 Indications for red cell transfusion in acute complications of sickle cell disease

| Top-up transfusion | Exchange transfusion |
|---|---|
| Transient red cell aplasia (usually parvovirus B19 infection) | Acute stroke |
| | Acute chest syndrome |
| Acute splenic or hepatic sequestration crisis | Severe sepsis |
| | Acute hepatic sequestration |
| | Acute multi-organ failure |

Table 8.3 Possible indications for elective red cell transfusion in severe sickle cell disease

| Supported by high-grade evidence from clinical trials | High-grade evidence currently unavailable |
|---|---|
| Primary stroke prevention (abnormal TCD in childhood) | Repeated severe painful crises |
| Secondary stroke prevention | Pulmonary hypertension |
| Major elective surgery | Fetal complications in pregnancy |
| Painful crises in pregnancy | Leg ulceration |

## 8.6.5   Red cell alloimmunisation in sickle cell disease

Alloimmunisation rates are high, exacerbated by differences in blood group distribution between patients with SCD and the predominantly white European blood donor population. Alloimmunisation rates of up to 57% have been reported after 200 transfusions. The majority of alloantibodies are to RhD, RhC and Kell. A significant proportion of SCD patients have the Ro phenotype (cDe) which is rare in donors of European origin. Serious Hazards of Transfusion (SHOT) reports show that transfusion reactions, especially acute or delayed haemolytic reactions, may be misinterpreted as sickle cell crises and treated inappropriately.

As with thalassaemic patients, preventing alloimmunisation to Rh and Kell appears to reduce the development of antibodies to other blood groups. Extended blood group phenotyping is ideally carried out before the first transfusion. If patients have already been transfused, molecular typing can be used. Donor red cells should be sickle Hb negative, and ideally less than 14 days old for top-up transfusions and 7 days old for exchange transfusions. At a minimum, transfused red cells should be matched for ABO, D, C, E, c, e and Kell.

It is often difficult to source fully compatible red cells in patients with multiple alloantibodies, especially when blood is required urgently. In that situation, the problem should be discussed with experts in transfusion medicine and blood group serology at the blood transfusion service, who will advise on the selection of the safest blood group combinations available in stock, taking into account the patient's current and historical antibodies and the urgency of transfusion. They will also initiate a search for fully compatible donations and advise on the management of possible haemolytic reactions. Many non-ABO antibodies typically cause delayed extravascular red cell destruction, which is less severe than ABO haemolysis. If the transfusion of red cells with a clinically significant incompatibility is unavoidable the clinical team should ensure the patient is adequately hydrated, and careful monitoring for evidence of haemolysis, including delayed reactions, is essential (see Chapter 5). If severe haemolysis occurs, or if the patient has had previous haemolytic reactions, options for treatment or prophylaxis include high-dose corticosteroids and intravenous immunoglobulin.

## 8.6.6   Hyperhaemolytic transfusion reactions

Hyperhaemolytic transfusion reactions (HHTRs) are characterised by destruction of both donor and recipient red cells after transfusion, often with a rapid and life-threatening fall in Hb concentration. Laboratory tests for red cell antibody-mediated haemolysis are usually negative. Patients usually present several days after the last transfusion and it may, initially, be diagnosed as an acute sickle cell crisis. Further transfusion may worsen the haemolysis and should be avoided if possible. Treatment with high-dose intravenous immunoglobulin has been effective in some reported cases but the benefits of corticosteroids are uncertain.

# 8.7 Transfusion in haemato-oncology

Many of the principles of transfusion management developed for these patients can be applied to patients with other cancers having treatment of similar intensity.

## 8.7.1 Transfusion support for myelosuppressive treatment

Intensive combination chemotherapy regimens for acute leukaemia and aggressive lymphoma, with or without haemopoietic stem cell (HSC) rescue, typically suppress the production of blood cells by the bone marrow for 7 to 14 days, during which the patient is likely to require prophylactic or therapeutic transfusions of red cells and platelets. Allogeneic (donor) HSC transplantation after myeloablative chemo-radiotherapy often requires much longer periods of transfusion support, particularly when recovery is complicated by delayed engraftment, acute graft-versus-host disease (GvHD) or severe sepsis.

## 8.7.2 Red cell transfusion

The ideal red cell 'transfusion trigger' for patients undergoing intensive cytotoxic therapy is uncertain. The patients have much in common with patients in critical care in which there is evidence to support a restrictive red cell transfusion policy (see Chapter 7). However, very low haematocrits may increase the risk of bleeding in patients with severe thrombocytopenia. In recent years, most units in the UK have followed a transfusion threshold of 80 or 90 g/L for patients without active bleeding.

## 8.7.3 Prophylactic platelet transfusion

It has long been standard practice to give prophylactic platelet transfusions to severely thrombocytopenic patients with the objective of preventing bleeding, especially serious or life-threatening bleeding such as intracerebral haemorrhage, although the evidence base for this is incomplete. Over the last decade, most units have used a platelet transfusion threshold of $10\times10^9$/L, largely based on an Italian trial comparing thresholds of 10 or $20\times10^9$/L. A randomised controlled trial in North America recently showed no significant difference in bleeding rates when patients on prophylaxis were randomised to low, medium or high platelet doses. Thus, there is no justification for the routine administration of 'double dose' platelets for prophylaxis.

Most trials of platelet therapy looking at dose or transfusion threshold have shown no difference in bleeding rates between the trial arms, and the routine use of prophylactic platelet transfusion has been questioned. Two recent large randomised controlled trials in haemato-oncology patients compared prophylactic platelet transfusion to a therapeutic policy based on a standardised daily assessment of bleeding and giving platelets only to those with a World Health Organization (WHO) clinically apparent haemorrhage greater than Grade 1 (WHO Grades range from Grade 1 (mild) to Grade 4 (debilitating/life-threatening)). Both trials showed an overall increase in Grade 2 to 4 bleeding in the no-prophylaxis group. However, the 14-centre UK/Australian TOPPS trial found that the subgroup of patients undergoing autologous HSC transplantation, with relatively short periods of thrombocytopenia, had similar bleeding rates in both treatment arms and platelet use was significantly lower in the no-prophylaxis group.

Although prophylactic platelets are beneficial in most patients receiving intensive chemotherapy they do not prevent all bleeding. Grade 2 to 4 haemorrhage occurred in 43% of patients receiving conventional prophylaxis in the TOPPS trial. Serious bleeds occur above the $10\times10^9$/L threshold and current research is investigating clinical and laboratory risk factors.

Based on current evidence:

- Prophylactic platelet transfusions should be given to patients receiving intensive chemotherapy, with a transfusion trigger of $10\times10^9$/L.
- One adult therapeutic dose (ATD) should be given once daily to adults and children >15 kg in weight (10–20 mL/kg in children and infants <15 kg).
- In a 70 kg adult, one ATD typically gives an immediate rise in platelet count of $20–40\times10^9$/L. The platelet increment can be measured as early as 10 minutes after completion of the transfusion.
- There is no rationale for the routine use of double dose platelets for prophylaxis.
- It is standard practice to increase the platelet transfusion threshold to $20\times10^9$/L in patients who are febrile and/or receiving antibiotic therapy for suspected bacterial or fungal infection, although there is no evidence from randomised trials to support this policy.
- A therapeutic platelet transfusion policy in patients undergoing lower risk procedures such as autologous HSC transplantation may be appropriate, but further research is required before this can be routinely recommended.
- Platelet prophylaxis is not required for bone marrow aspiration or trephine biopsy, but local pressure should be applied.
- For patients requiring lumbar puncture, central-line insertion, percutaneous organ biopsies and most invasive surgeries the platelet count should be increased to >$50\times10^9$/L. For adults and children >15 kg, one ATD of platelets should be administered shortly before the procedure and a post-transfusion platelet count should be checked to confirm the count has risen to the desired level.
- There is no evidence to support the practice of once or twice weekly prophylactic platelet transfusions in non-bleeding patients with chronic severe thrombocytopenia.

## 8.7.4    Refractoriness to platelet transfusion

'Refractoriness' is the repeated failure to obtain a satisfactory response to platelet transfusion. Control of bleeding is the most clinically relevant marker but, in practice, it is usual to measure the increase in platelet count after transfusion. Formulas to derive platelet recovery or corrected count increment are of limited value outside research as they require knowledge of the platelet content of each unit transfused. In the clinical setting, simpler indicators, such as failure of the immediately post-transfusion (10 to 60 minutes) platelet increment to exceed the transfusion trigger or a rise of less than $10\times10^9$/L 20 to 24 hours after transfusion, are used. The diagnosis of refractoriness should only be made after an unsatisfactory response to two or more transfusions. Platelet refractoriness can be due to immunological or, more commonly, non-immunological causes associated with increased platelet consumption or losses (Table 8.4).

8 Effective transfusion

99

### Table 8.4 Causes of platelet refractoriness

| Immunological causes | Non-immunological causes |
|---|---|
| Antibodies to antigens on platelets (HLA, HPA, ABO) | Infection |
| Platelet autoantibodies | Antibiotics (amphotericin B and fluoroquinolones) |
| Drug-dependent antibodies | Splenomegaly/hypersplenism |
| Immune complexes | Disseminated intravascular coagulation (DIC) |
| | Platelet loss due to bleeding |

Platelet refractoriness due to human leucocyte antigen (HLA) alloimmunisation has been less common since universal leucodepletion of blood components was introduced. The typical patient is now a female sensitised by previous pregnancy. If a non-immunological cause has been excluded, the patient should be screened for HLA antibodies after discussion with a transfusion medicine specialist. The presence of HLA antibodies does not prove immunological refractoriness but the response to platelet transfusion from donors matched, as closely as possible, for the patient's HLA-A and HLA-B antigens should be assessed. The UK Transfusion Services have panels of HLA-typed donors. ABO-compatible platelets should be used wherever possible and HLA-matched platelet transfusions should be irradiated to prevent transfusion-associated graft-versus-host disease. Immediate (10 to 60 minutes) and 24-hour post-transfusion platelet increments should be measured. If a satisfactory response is seen, HLA-matched platelet transfusions should be continued as long as compatible donors are available. HLA antibodies may reduce or disappear during treatment and it may be helpful to repeat the HLA-antibody screen monthly during treatment. If there is no response to HLA-matched platelets it is reasonable to screen for human platelet antigen (HPA) and other less common antibodies after specialist advice.

## 8.7.5 Selection of compatible blood for patients who have received a marrow or peripheral blood HSC transplant from an ABO or RhD-incompatible donor

Up to 25% of HLA-identical sibling donor/recipient pairs have different ABO blood groups (Table 8.5). SHOT reports show that component selection errors for patients who have changed blood group after allogeneic HSC transplant are common and often stem from poor communication between the clinical team and transfusion laboratory or when there is shared care between different hospitals. A clear post-transplant transfusion policy should be developed for all transplant patients and circulated to the clinical and laboratory teams involved in their care. The recommended ABO groups for components transfused in the immediate post-transplant period are shown in Table 8.6.

Haemolysis due to ABO incompatibility may occur immediately on stem cell infusion (usually with bone marrow transplants that are heavily contaminated with red cells) or be delayed for 7 to 14 days due to production of antibodies by residual host or transplanted lymphocytes (more common with peripheral blood-derived HSC). It is occasionally life threatening. In RhD-incompatible transplants, the main risk is delayed haemolysis where the donor is RhD negative and the recipient RhD positive.

## Table 8.5 Categories of ABO-incompatible HSC transplant

| | |
|---|---|
| Major ABO incompatibility | The recipient's plasma contains anti-A, anti-B or anti-A,B antibodies that are incompatible with donor red cells (e.g. group A donor and group O recipient) |
| Minor ABO incompatibility | The donor's plasma contains anti-A, anti-B or anti-A,B antibodies that can react with the recipient's red cells (e.g. donor group O and recipient group A) |
| Bidirectional ABO incompatibility | Both the donor and recipient's plasma contain anti-A, anti-B or anti-A,B antibodies reactive with recipient and donor red cells respectively (e.g. donor group A and recipient group B) |

Immediate haemolysis in major ABO mismatch marrow transplants can be prevented by red cell depletion of the marrow harvest. This is unnecessary with peripheral blood HSC transplants that contain <10 mL red cells. In minor ABO mismatch marrow transplants the harvest can be plasma depleted to remove high-titre donor anti-A or -B (this is unnecessary in peripheral blood HSC transplants where the small amount of plasma is rapidly diluted after infusion).

## Table 8.6 Recommended ABO blood group of components transfused in the early post-transplant period

| | Donor | Recipient | Red cells | Platelets | FFP |
|---|---|---|---|---|---|
| Major ABO incompatibility | A | O | O | A | A |
| | B | O | O | B | B |
| | AB | O | O | A | AB |
| | AB | A | A$^a$ | A | AB |
| | AB | B | B$^a$ | B | AB |
| Minor ABO incompatibility | O | A | O | A | A |
| | O | B | O | B | B |
| | O | AB | O | A | AB |
| | A | AB | A$^a$ | A | AB |
| | B | AB | B$^a$ | B | AB |
| Bidirectional ABO incompatibility | A | B | O | B | AB |
| | B | A | O | A | AB |

[a] Group O red cells may also be used.

Once conversion to donor blood group is complete, components of that group can be given. In both major and minor RhD mismatch, RhD negative red cells and platelets are given post-transplant. If, for reasons of availability, RhD positive platelets have to be given to unsensitised RhD negative recipients, 250 IU of anti-D immunoglobulin subcutaneously will cover up to five adult therapeutic doses of platelets over a 5-week period.

## 8.7.6 Prevention of transfusion-associated graft-versus-host disease (TA-GvHD)

This fatal complication can be prevented by the use of irradiated cellular blood components (red cells, platelets and granulocytes) in patients at high risk (see Chapter 5 for a more detailed discussion of TA-GvHD and prophylaxis). It is not necessary to irradiate red cells or platelets for adults or children with acute leukaemia except for HLA-selected platelets or donations from first or second degree relatives. The 2010 British Committee for Standards in Haematology (BCSH) guideline on the use of irradiated blood components (http://www.bcshguidelines.com) recommendations for transfusion of irradiated components in haemato-oncology patients are summarised in Table 8.7. The guidelines are regularly reviewed as new immunosuppressive drugs and biologicals are introduced into practice and evidence of risk accumulates. For example, irradiated components are currently recommended for patients, including solid organ transplant recipients, treated with the lymphocyte-depleting monoclonal antibody alemtuzumab (anti-CD52) but not for those receiving rituximab (anti-CD20).

**Table 8.7 Indications for irradiated cellular blood components[a] in haemato-oncology patients**

| Patient group | Irradiated blood components |
|---|---|
| Adults or children with acute leukaemia | Not required (except for HLA-selected platelets or donations from first or second degree relatives) |
| Recipients of allogeneic (donor) HSC transplantation | From the start of conditioning chemo-radiotherapy. Continue while receiving GvHD prophylaxis (usually for 6 months post-transplant) |
| | If chronic GvHD or on immunosuppressive treatment, continue irradiated blood components |
| Bone marrow and peripheral blood stem cell donors | Provide irradiated cellular components during and for 7 days before the harvest |
| Bone marrow or peripheral blood HSC harvesting for future autologous reinfusion | Provide irradiated cellular components during and for 7 days before the harvest |
| Autologous HSC transplant patients | From start of conditioning chemo-radiotherapy until 3 months post-transplant (6 months if total body irradiation was used) |
| Adults and children with Hodgkin lymphoma at any stage of the disease | Irradiated cellular components indefinitely |
| Patients treated with purine analogues (fludarabine, cladribine and deoxycoformicin)[b] | Irradiated cellular components indefinitely |
| Patients treated with alemtuzumab (anti-CD52) therapy[c] | Irradiated cellular components indefinitely |

[a] Red cells, platelets and granulocytes

[b] Irradiated components are recommended for newer purine analogues and related compounds, such as bendamustine, until further data are available

[c] Irradiated components are also recommended for solid organ transplant patients receiving alemtuzumab

Patients at risk of TA-GvHD should be given clear written information. Patient information leaflets, cards and warning stickers for the hospital notes are available from the UK Blood Services. SHOT annual reports show that failure to prescribe or administer irradiated components is a common cause of incorrect blood component transfused incidents. Many of these are due to poor communication between clinical teams, transfusion laboratories and shared-care hospitals. SHOT (http://www.shotuk.org) has made a series of recommendations concerning better clinical communication and documentation, and improved laboratory and clinical information systems (including IT links with pharmacy and diagnostic services), which should be incorporated into local policies and regularly audited.

### 8.7.7 Prevention of cytomegalovirus transmission by transfusion

Cytomegalovirus (CMV) can be transmitted by cellular blood components and may produce fatal infection in immunocompromised patients, especially allogeneic HSC transplant recipients. The risk can be reduced by blood donor CMV antibody screening (CMV negative components) or pre-storage leucocyte-depleted blood. Current evidence-based recommendations for different patient groups are discussed in detail in Chapter 5. In summary, standard pre-storage leucodepleted components are suitable for adult and paediatric HSC transplant patients.

### 8.7.8 Long-term transfusion support for patients with myelodysplasia

There are increasing numbers of elderly patients with 'low-risk' myelodysplasia who are transfusion dependent for months or years. Tolerance of anaemia varies widely between patients and severe fatigue is a commonly reported symptom. Transfusion plans in individual patients should be designed to minimise symptoms of anaemia and improve health-related quality of life rather than achieve an arbitrary Hb concentration. For example, some patients may benefit from higher mean Hb levels and others from smaller, more frequent transfusions to prevent wide fluctuations in Hb concentration. Transfusion triggers designed for perioperative or critical care patients are unlikely to be appropriate.

Up to 16% of patients eventually become alloimmunised to red cell antigens and this may be delayed by selecting Rh and K-compatible donations. Long-term transfusion is also associated with transfusional haemosiderosis and organ damage due to iron overload. Chelation therapy with agents such as desferrioxamine may be indicated in selected patients, carefully balancing the benefits against impairment of quality of life from frequent overnight subcutaneous infusions.

# 8.8 Indications for intravenous immunoglobulin (IVIg)

Human normal immunoglobulin products are manufactured from large pools of donor plasma. All the products used in the UK are imported as a variant Creutzfeldt–Jakob disease (vCJD) risk-reduction measure. The two main uses for IVIg are as replacement therapy in primary or acquired antibody deficiency disorders and as immunomodulatory agents in patients with autoimmune or inflammatory conditions. Because of limitations on supply of IVIg, the UK Departments of Health have commissioned evidence-based clinical guidelines to prioritise its use. Tables 8.8 and 8.9 are based on the 2011 update of these guidelines.

8 Effective transfusion

**Table 8.8 High-priority ('red') indications for intravenous immunoglobulin – an adequate evidence base and potentially life-saving**

| Primary and secondary antibody deficiency states | Primary immunodeficiencies |
| --- | --- |
| | Thymoma with immunodeficiency |
| | HSC transplant in primary immunodeficiencies |
| | Specific antibody deficiency |
| Haematology | Alloimmune thrombocytopenia (feto-maternal/neonatal) |
| | Haemolytic disease of the newborn |
| | Idiopathic thrombocytopenic purpura (ITP) – acute and persistent |
| Neurology | Chronic inflammatory demyelinating polyradiculoneuropathy (acute) |
| | Guillain–Barré syndrome |
| | Paraprotein-associated demyelinating neuropathy |
| Others | Kawasaki disease |
| | Toxic epidermal necrolysis |

**Table 8.9 'Blue' indications for intravenous immunoglobulin – a reasonable evidence base but other treatment options are available**

| Primary and secondary antibody deficiency states | Secondary antibody deficiency (any cause) |
| --- | --- |
| Haematology | Acquired red cell aplasia |
| | Autoimmune haemolytic anaemia |
| | Clotting factor inhibitors |
| | Haemophagocytic syndrome |
| | Post-transfusion purpura |
| Neurology | Chronic inflammatory demyelinating polyradiculoneuropathy (chronic) |
| | Inflammatory myelopathies |
| | Myasthenia gravis |
| | Multifocal motor neuropathy |
| | Rasmussen syndrome |
| | Stiff person syndrome |
| Others | Autoimmune congenital heart block |
| | Autoimmune uveitis |
| | Immunobullous diseases |
| | Necrotising staphylococcal sepsis |
| | Severe or recurrent *Clostridium difficile* colitis |
| | Staphylococcal or streptococcal toxic shock syndrome |
| | Antibody-mediated rejection after solid organ transplantation |

# EFFECTIVE TRANSFUSION IN
# OBSTETRIC PRACTICE

# Essentials

- Inappropriate transfusions during pregnancy and the postpartum period expose the mother to the risk of haemolytic disease of the fetus and newborn (HDFN) in subsequent pregnancies.
- Prevention and treatment of anaemia in pregnancy (most commonly due to iron deficiency) avoids unnecessary blood transfusion.
- A blood count should be checked at the antenatal booking visit and at 28 weeks (allowing sufficient time to treat iron deficiency before delivery).
- Oral iron replacement is appropriate for most patients, but intravenous iron (after the first trimester) may produce a more rapid response and should be used in women intolerant of oral iron.
- Transfusion is rarely required in haemodynamically stable pregnant women with Hb >70 or 80 g/L unless there is active (or a high risk of) bleeding.
- Cytomegalovirus (CMV) seronegative red cells should be provided for elective transfusions in pregnancy but standard, leucodepleted units may be used in an emergency to avoid delay.
- Major obstetric haemorrhage remains an important cause of maternal death. Successful management depends on well-rehearsed multidisciplinary protocols, rapid access to red cells (including emergency group O negative units) and excellent communication with the transfusion laboratory. Access to cell salvage reduces use of donor blood and early administration of tranexamic acid may reduce mortality.
- Pregnancies potentially affected by HDFN should be managed by specialist teams with facilities for early diagnosis, intrauterine transfusion and support of high-dependency neonates.
- Alloimmunisation of RhD negative women is the most important cause of HDFN. It was a major cause of perinatal mortality before routine postnatal anti-D Ig prophylaxis was introduced.
- Women may be alloimmunised by feto-maternal haemorrhage during pregnancy or at delivery, or by blood transfusion.
- Anti-D Ig should be administered within 72 hours of delivery of a RhD positive baby or a potentially sensitising event in pregnancy in accordance with national guidelines.
- The incidence of HDFN has been further reduced by the addition of routine antenatal anti-D prophylaxis (RAADP).

# 9.1   Normal haematological values in pregnancy

During normal pregnancy, physiological changes in the mother affect the reference range for haematological parameters. Knowledge of these changes helps to avoid unnecessary blood transfusions caused by misinterpretation of blood count results:

- Maternal plasma volume increases by around 50% above the non-pregnant value by the late second trimester. Red cell mass only increases by 25–30%, resulting in a fall in Hb concentration ('physiological anaemia of pregnancy').
- Up to 10% of healthy pregnant women have a count below the non-pregnant reference range of 150–400×10$^9$/L at term ('gestational thrombocytopenia'). The count rarely falls below 100×10$^9$/L and there is no increase in bleeding risk.

■ Many coagulation factors, including plasma fibrinogen and Factor VIIIc, are increased in normal pregnancy and the anticoagulant factor Protein S is reduced. This contributes to the increased risk of thrombotic complications in pregnancy.

# 9.2   Anaemia and pregnancy

Prevention of anaemia in pregnancy is important in avoiding unnecessary blood transfusion. The World Health Organization (WHO) defines anaemia in pregnant women as Hb <110 g/L and postpartum anaemia as Hb <100 g/L. Taking account of the physiological changes in Hb concentration during pregnancy, the 2011 British Committee for Standards in Haematology (BCSH) *UK Guidelines on the Management of Iron Deficiency in Pregnancy* (http://www.bcshguidelines.com) recommend the following thresholds for investigation of anaemia:

■ First trimester: Hb <110 g/L
■ Second and third trimesters: Hb <105 g/L
■ Postpartum: Hb <100 g/L.

## 9.2.1   Iron deficiency

This is the most common cause of anaemia in pregnancy. At least 30% of UK women have absent iron stores at the onset of pregnancy due to menstrual bleeding and suboptimal dietary intake. Babies born to iron-deficient mothers are more likely to be anaemic in the first 3 months of life and have a higher risk of abnormal psychomotor development. Severe maternal iron deficiency, common in less developed countries, may cause increased risk of preterm delivery and low birth weight. Iron-deficient mothers often have increased fatigue, poor concentration and emotional disturbance. After delivery, this may impair the ability to look after the newborn and prevent successful initiation of breastfeeding.

A routine full blood count should be carried out at the antenatal booking visit and at 28 weeks (allowing sufficient time to treat iron deficiency before delivery). Serum ferritin levels <15 µg/L are diagnostic of absent iron stores and a level <30 µg/L should prompt iron supplementation.

### 9.2.1.1   Treatment of iron deficiency anaemia in pregnancy

Dietary changes are not sufficient to correct iron deficiency in pregnancy. Oral iron supplements are the first choice, with a therapeutic dose of 100 to 200 mg elemental iron daily (e.g. ferrous sulphate or ferrous fumarate 200 mg two or three times daily). The Hb concentration should increase by around 20 g/L over 3 to 4 weeks and iron should be continued for 3 months after the Hb returns to normal (and at least 6 weeks postpartum) to replenish iron stores.

Many women are intolerant of oral iron because of gastric irritation and diarrhoea or constipation. If a reduction in oral iron dose is not effective, then treatment with parenteral iron should be considered. Modern intravenous iron preparations (see Chapter 6) are safe after the first trimester and may produce a faster and more complete response than oral iron. They are particularly useful when anaemia is diagnosed late in pregnancy. The ability to give a single total replacement dose makes it possible to treat postpartum iron deficiency anaemia before the mother leaves hospital.

### 9.2.2 Folate deficiency

Anaemia due to folate deficiency is less common and usually reflects poor dietary intake of fresh fruit and leafy vegetables. Other causes include malabsorption (most commonly coeliac disease) or increased requirements in haemolytic anaemia or haemoglobinopathies. Folate deficiency typically produces a macrocytic anaemia (large red blood cells – increased mean cell volume (MCV) on full blood count). Treatment is with oral folic acid 5 mg daily.

# 9.3    Red cell transfusion in pregnancy

Clinical audits show that many transfusions in pregnancy, especially in the postpartum period, are inappropriate and could be prevented by better antenatal monitoring and the targeted use of iron supplements. Transfusion exposes women to the risk of sensitisation to red cell antigens and haemolytic disease of the fetus and newborn (HDFN) in subsequent pregnancies. In the absence of major haemorrhage, the decision to transfuse should be made after careful clinical assessment rather than on the basis of a specific Hb concentration. Clinically stable, healthy women with Hb >70 or 80 g/L can usually be managed with oral or parenteral iron. Transfusion should be reserved for women with continued bleeding (or at risk of further significant haemorrhage), severe symptoms that need immediate correction or evidence of cardiac decompensation.

Obstetric units should have agreed local guidelines for red cell transfusion in women who are not actively bleeding. Cytomegalovirus (CMV) seronegative red cells should be provided, where possible, for pregnant women. In an emergency, such as major haemorrhage, standard leucocyte-depleted components should be given to avoid delay.

# 9.4    Major obstetric haemorrhage

Blood flow to the uterus is around 700 mL/minute at term and bleeding can be dramatic and rapidly fatal. Risk factors for obstetric haemorrhage include placenta praevia, placental abruption and postpartum haemorrhage (most commonly due to uterine atony). Obstetric haemorrhage is a major problem in less developed countries, responsible for half of the approximately 500 000 maternal deaths each year across the world. Major haemorrhage remains an important cause of maternal mortality in the UK, with an incidence of 3.7 per 1000 births and nine deaths in 2006–2008. Analysis by the UK Centre for Maternal and Child Enquiries (CMACE) (http://onlinelibrary.wiley.com/doi/10.1111/j.1471-0528.2010.02847.x/pdf) shows that the management of fatal cases was often suboptimal with underestimation of the degree of haemorrhage and poor team working. The Centre emphasises the need for:

■ Clear local policies
■ Training of front-line staff
■ Multidisciplinary team working
■ Regular 'fire drills'
■ Excellent communication with the blood transfusion laboratory.

Obstetric haemorrhage is often complicated by disseminated intravascular coagulation (DIC) and defibrination. The primary treatment is evacuation of the uterine contents but supportive therapy with fresh frozen plasma (FFP), cryoprecipitate (or fibrinogen concentrate) and platelet transfusion is often required. There is increasing evidence that the antifibrinolytic agent, tranexamic acid, can significantly reduce mortality in major obstetric haemorrhage and this is being explored in a large international randomised trial (the WOMAN trial – http://www.thewomantrial.lshtm.ac.uk/).

The Royal College of Obstetricians and Gynaecologists has produced guidelines on the prevention and management of postpartum haemorrhage (http://www.rcog.org.uk/womens-health/clinical-guidance/prevention-and-management-postpartum-haemorrhage-green-top-52). Obstetric and anaesthetic staff of appropriate seniority must be involved and access to expert haematological advice is important. Transfusion support for patients with major obstetric haemorrhage should follow the basic principles discussed in Chapter 7. There must be rapid access to compatible red cells and blood components, including emergency group O RhD negative blood. Use of intraoperative cell salvage (ICS) by teams experienced in the technique reduces exposure to donor red cells and can be life-saving, especially in women who decline allogeneic blood transfusion. Use of ICS in obstetrics is endorsed by the National Institute for Health and Care Excellence (NICE). Salvaged blood should be transfused through a leucodepletion filter (see Chapter 6).

The dose of tranexamic acid used in the WOMAN trial is 1g by intravenous injection as soon as possible; a second dose is given if bleeding persists after 30 minutes or recurs within the first 24 hours.

# 9.5 Prevention of haemolytic disease of the fetus and newborn (HDFN)

**Pregnancies potentially affected by HDFN should be cared for by specialist teams with facilities for early diagnosis, intrauterine transfusion and support of high-dependency neonates.**

HDFN occurs when the mother has IgG red cell alloantibodies in her plasma that cross the placenta and bind to fetal red cells possessing the corresponding antigen. Immune haemolysis may then cause variable degrees of fetal anaemia; in the most severe cases the fetus may die of heart failure in utero (hydrops fetalis). After delivery, affected babies may develop jaundice due to high unconjugated bilirubin levels and are at risk of neurological damage. The three most important red cell alloantibodies in clinical practice are to RhD (anti-D), Rhc (anti-c) and Kell (anti-K). The major effect of anti-K is suppression of red cell production in the fetus, rather than haemolysis.

Red cell alloantibodies in the mother occur as a result of previous pregnancies (where fetal red cells containing paternal blood group antigens cross the placenta) or blood transfusion. Naturally occurring IgG anti-A or anti-B antibodies in a group O mother can cross the placenta but rarely cause more than mild jaundice and anaemia in the neonate (ABO haemolytic disease). Recommendations for serological screening for maternal red cell antibodies in pregnancy are summarised in Table 9.1 (see also BCSH *Guideline for Blood Grouping and Antibody Testing in Pregnancy* – http://www.bcshguidelines.com). Knowledge of any maternal red cell alloantibodies is also important in providing compatible blood without delay in the event of obstetric haemorrhage.

### Table 9.1 Screening for maternal red cell alloantibodies in pregnancy

At booking visit (12–16 weeks gestation) – maternal blood sample for ABO and Rh group and red cell alloantibody screen.

If an alloantibody capable of causing HDFN is detected (e.g. anti-D, c or K):

- Confirm in red cell reference laboratory, issue an Antibody Card to the mother and seek specialist clinical advice.
- Determining the father's phenotype helps to predict the likelihood of a fetus carrying the relevant red cell antigen (but note issues around establishing paternity).
- The fetal genotype can now be determined by polymerase chain reaction on trace amounts of free fetal DNA in the mother's circulation. This is currently highly sensitive for RhD, C, c, E, e and Kell.

Antenatal patients with anti-D, anti-c or anti-K should have regular repeat testing during the second trimester to monitor the antibody concentration:

- Usually every 4 weeks to 28 weeks gestation then every 2 weeks to term.
- Referral to a fetal medicine specialist is recommended once anti-D levels are >4 IU/mL, anti-c >7.5 IU/mL and in any woman with anti-K (as the severity of fetal anaemia is unpredictable).

All other women (both RhD positive and negative) should have repeat antibody screening at 28 weeks gestation (prior to RAADP) to exclude late development of red cell alloantibodies.

## 9.5.1 HDFN due to anti-D

This is the most important cause of HDFN and may occur in RhD negative women carrying a RhD positive fetus. Around 15% of white Europeans are RhD negative. Typically, the mother is sensitised by the transplacental passage of RhD positive fetal red cells during a previous pregnancy – usually at delivery or during the third trimester. HDFN then occurs in subsequent RhD positive pregnancies when further exposure to fetal red cells causes a secondary immune response and increased levels of maternal IgG anti-RhD alloantibodies that can cross the placenta. Before the introduction of routine postnatal prophylaxis with anti-RhD immunoglobulin (anti-D Ig, standard dose 500 IU) in the 1970s, HDFN was a major cause of perinatal mortality in the UK (46/100 000 births). Rates of sensitisation fell further with the introduction of routine antenatal anti-D prophylaxis in the third trimester (RAADP) and mortality is now <1.6/100 000 births.

## 9.5.2 Potentially sensitising events

RhD negative mothers can also produce anti-RhD in response to potentially sensitising events that may cause feto-maternal haemorrhage (FMH) during pregnancy or by blood transfusion. The BCSH *Guideline for the Use of Anti-D Immunoglobulin for the Prevention of Haemolytic Disease of the Fetus and Newborn* 2013 lists the following as potentially sensitising events in pregnancy:

- Amniocentesis, chorionic villus biopsy and cordocentesis
- Antepartum haemorrhage/vaginal bleeding in pregnancy
- External cephalic version
- Fall or abdominal trauma
- Ectopic pregnancy
- Evacuation of molar pregnancy
- Intrauterine death and stillbirth
- In utero therapeutic interventions (transfusion, surgery, insertion of shunts, laser)
- Miscarriage, threatened miscarriage

9 Effective transfusion in obstetric practice

- Therapeutic termination of pregnancy
- Delivery – normal, instrumental or Caesarean section
- Intraoperative cell salvage.

Recommendations for the administration of prophylactic anti-D Ig for potentially sensitising events are summarised in Table 9.2 and the reader is referred to the current BCSH *Guideline for the Use of Anti-D Immunoglobulin for the Prevention of Haemolytic Disease of the Fetus and Newborn* (http://www.bcshguidelines.com) and the Royal College of Obstetricians and Gynaecologists' Green Top Guideline No. 22 on the use of anti-D immunoglobulin for Rhesus D prophylaxis (http://www.rcog.org.uk/files/rcog-corp/GTG22AntiDJuly2013.pdf) for up-to-date guidance. An intramuscular (IM) injection of 125 IU anti-D Ig, or 100 IU of the appropriate preparation given intravenously (IV), 'covers' a FMH of 1 mL red cells. Women with anomalous RhD typing results should be treated as RhD negative until confirmatory testing is completed. Anti-D Ig should be administered within 72 hours of the potentially sensitising event (although some benefit may occur up to 10 days if treatment is inadvertently delayed).

If the pregnancy has reached 20 weeks or more, administration of anti-D Ig should be accompanied by a test on the mother's blood to estimate the volume of fetal red cells that have entered the maternal circulation (e.g. Kleihauer test) in case it exceeds that covered by the standard dose of anti-D Ig. The Kleihauer test detects fetal cells, which contain HbF, in the maternal blood. If the screening Kleihauer test suggests a FMH >2 mL then the FMH volume should be confirmed by flow cytometry, which accurately measures the population of RhD positive cells. Detailed guidance is given in the 2009 BCSH *Guidelines on the Estimation of Fetomaternal Haemorrhage* (http://www.bcshguidelines.com).

For recurrent or intermittent uterine bleeding, a minimum of 500 IU anti-D Ig should be given at 6-weekly intervals. Estimation of FMH haemorrhage by the Kleihauer technique should be carried out at 2-weekly intervals and additional anti-D Ig administered if required.

**Table 9.2 Anti-D Ig for potentially sensitising events in pregnancy**

| <12 weeks | 12–20 weeks | 20+ weeks |
|---|---|---|
| At least 250 IU anti-D Ig if:<br>• surgical intervention<br>• termination of pregnancy (surgical or medical)<br>• unusually heavy bleeding<br>• unusually severe pain<br>• unsure of gestation<br>Kleihauer test not required | At least 250 IU anti-D Ig<br>Kleihauer test not required | At least 500 IU anti-D Ig<br>Take maternal blood for Kleihauer test<br>Further anti-D Ig if indicated by Kleihauer results |

## 9.5.3 Routine antenatal anti-D prophylaxis (RAADP)

RAADP should be offered to all RhD negative, non-sensitised women. They should be supplied with clear written information and informed consent should be obtained. Both two-dose (at 28 and 34 weeks) and larger single-dose (at 28–30 weeks) prophylactic anti-D regimens reduce maternal sensitisation but there are no comparative data to confirm their relative efficacy. The single-dose regimen may achieve better compliance but anti-D levels at term may be low in some women.

Recommended anti-D Ig doses for RAADP:

- Two-dose regimen – minimum of 500 IU at 28 and 34 weeks.
- Single-dose regimen – 1500 IU at 28–30 weeks.

RAADP should be given even if the woman has received anti-D Ig prophylaxis for a potentially sensitising event earlier in the pregnancy. The transfusion laboratory should be informed of the administration of RAADP in case the woman requires pre-transfusion testing. It is not possible to differentiate between 'prophylactic' and 'immune' (allo-) anti-D in maternal blood in laboratory tests.

### 9.5.4 Anti-D Ig prophylaxis after the birth of a RhD positive baby or intrauterine death

Following the birth of a child to a RhD negative woman, a cord blood sample should be tested to determine the baby's ABO and Rh group. If the cord Rh group is unclear, or if a sample cannot be obtained, the baby should be assumed to be RhD positive for anti-D Ig administration purposes. A direct antiglobulin test (DAT) on the cord sample should only be performed if HDFN is suspected.

**If the baby is RhD positive, a minimum of 500 IU anti-D Ig should be administered to non-sensitised RhD negative women, within 72 hours of the birth.**

A maternal blood sample for confirmation of her ABO and RhD status and for FMH screening should be taken within 2 hours of delivery. A dose of 500 IU anti-D Ig given IM will cover a FMH of up to 4 mL. If an additional dose is required, it should be based on 125 IU/mL fetal red cells if given IM or 100 IU/mL if given IV (manufacturer's instructions on dosing should be followed and anti-D Ig produced for IM use only must not be given IV). If a FMH of >4 mL is detected, follow-up maternal blood samples should be tested 72 hours after an IM dose (48 hours if given IV) to confirm clearance of fetal red cells from the maternal circulation. In the case of very large FMH, administration of IV anti-D Ig may be more convenient and less painful than large-volume or repeated IM administration. If anti-D Ig is inadvertently omitted, there may be some benefit in giving prophylaxis up to 10 days.

If intraoperative cell salvage is used at Caesarean section, 1500 IU anti-D Ig should be administered immediately after the procedure if the baby is RhD positive and maternal FMH screening should be performed.

### 9.5.5 Inadvertent transfusion of RhD positive blood

If RhD positive blood is inadvertently transfused to a non-sensitised RhD negative woman of child-bearing potential, the advice of a transfusion medicine specialist should be obtained and the appropriate dose of anti-D Ig administered (125 IU/mL fetal red cells if given IM or 100 IU/mL IV). For transfusions >15 mL, IV anti-D Ig is more practical. FMH testing should be carried out at 48-hour intervals and further anti-D Ig given until clearance of fetal cells is confirmed. If more than one unit of red cells has been transfused, red cell exchange should be considered to reduce the load of RhD positive cells and the dose of anti-D Ig required.

9 Effective transfusion in obstetric practice

# 10

# EFFECTIVE TRANSFUSION IN PAEDIATRIC PRACTICE

# Essentials

- The potential risks and benefits must always be considered when making the decision to transfuse children but there is a lack of high-quality research evidence on which to base guidelines.
- SHOT has reported a higher incidence of serious adverse events related to transfusion in children (including identification errors).
- Children transfused in fetal or neonatal life have the longest potential lifespan in which to develop late adverse effects of transfusion.
- Extra safety measures for blood components for fetal, neonatal and infant transfusion include enhanced donor selection and screening for clinically significant blood group antibodies (paediatric antibody tests or 'PAnTs').
- Fresh frozen plasma (FFP) and cryoprecipitate for all patients born on or after 1 January 1996 is imported from countries with a low risk of variant Creutzfeldt–Jakob disease (vCJD) and is pathogen-inactivated.
- Transfusion volumes and rates for children should be carefully calculated and prescribed in mL, not component units, to minimise dosing errors and reduce the risk of circulatory overload.
- Intrauterine transfusion of red cells (for haemolytic disease of the fetus and newborn (HDFN)) or platelets (for neonatal alloimmune thrombocytopenia (NAIT)) and neonatal exchange transfusion are complex procedures requiring multidisciplinary input. They should only be performed in specialist units.
- Randomised controlled trials suggest that restrictive Hb transfusion thresholds (similar to current UK guidelines) are safe in clinically stable neonates requiring small volume 'top-up' transfusions. However, there is still uncertainty, especially about long-term outcomes, and further research is needed.
- Low platelet counts are common in sick neonates but the relationship of thrombocytopenia to serious bleeding and appropriate triggers for platelet prophylaxis remain uncertain.
- A significant proportion of FFP transfusions in patients in neonatal intensive care units (NICUs) and paediatric intensive care units (PICUs) are given to non-bleeding patients with minor abnormalities in coagulation parameters of uncertain significance.
- A restrictive red cell transfusion policy (threshold 70g/L) is safe for clinically stable children on PICUs.
- Guidelines for the transfusion management of haemato-oncology patients are similar to adult guidelines, although a more liberal platelet prophylaxis policy may be justified.
- Transfusion management of major haemorrhage in children is largely based on experience with adult patients. Age-specific blood components should be used as long as urgent provision of blood is not delayed. Tranexamic acid is now recommended for children with major traumatic haemorrhage.

Paediatric transfusion is a complex area of medicine covering a wide age range from intrauterine life to young adults. The prescriber must balance the risks and benefits of transfusion in each age group and be aware of the indications for special components. However, compared to adult practice there is a relative lack of high-quality research to inform evidence-based guidelines. The UK *National Comparative Audit of the Use of Red*

10 Effective transfusion in paediatric practice

*Cells in Neonates and Children 2010* (http://hospital.blood.co.uk/library/pdf/NCA_red_cells_ neonates_children.pdf) showed that 74% of transfused patients received a single red cell component during their admission, suggesting that many transfusions might be avoidable.

The Serious Hazards of Transfusion (SHOT) initiative has reported a higher rate of adverse events in children, including identification errors, especially in the first year of life. Identification errors include confusion of maternal and neonatal samples, problems with multiple births, and failure to apply (or maintain) identification bands. Extra blood component safety measures have been developed for individuals transfused in fetal or neonatal life who have the longest potential lifespan in which to develop late adverse effects of transfusion. Components for fetal, neonatal and infant transfusion are collected from previously tested donors who have given at least one donation in the last two years. These components are screened for clinically significant blood group antibodies (including high-titre anti-A and anti-B) and an indirect antiglobulin test is performed – often known as 'PAnTs' (paediatric antibody tests). Fresh frozen plasma (FFP) and cryoprecipitate for all patients born on or after 1 January 1996 is imported from countries with a low risk of vCJD and is pathogen-inactivated (methylene blue or solvent detergent – see Chapter 3).

# 10.1 Fetal transfusion

The most common indications for intrauterine transfusion (IUT) are red cells for prevention and treatment of fetal anaemia due to haemolytic disease of the fetus and newborn (HDFN) or parvovirus infection and platelets for neonatal alloimmune thrombocytopenia (NAIT). This is a highly specialised area of medical practice requiring close collaboration between experts in fetal medicine, haematology and blood transfusion, and rapid access to blood counting. Even in the most expert hands IUT carries a risk of fetal death of 1–3% per procedure and fetomaternal haemorrhage may cause further sensitisation and worsening of HDFN.

## 10.1.1 Intrauterine transfusion of red cells for HDFN

Maternal aspects of the management of HDFN are covered in Chapter 9. The objective of red cell IUT is to prevent or treat life-threatening fetal anaemia (hydrops fetalis) and allow the pregnancy to continue to a stage where a viable baby can be delivered (ideally at least 36 weeks gestation). High-risk pregnancies are monitored by weekly fetal Doppler ultrasound scans to measure middle cerebral artery peak systolic velocity, an indication of the severity of fetal anaemia, and regular ultrasound monitoring of fetal growth. Fetal blood sampling is indicated if severe anaemia before 24 weeks gestation is suspected, if there has been a previous intrauterine death, or if there is a rapid increase in maternal red cell alloantibody levels.

Guidelines for IUT vary between specialist units but published indications include a haematocrit of <0.25 between 18 and 26 weeks of gestation and <0.3 after 26 weeks. The target haematocrit after IUT is usually around 0.45. To balance the competing risks of fetal anaemia and the hazards of invasive IUT procedures, the transfusion programme is started as late as possible and the frequency of transfusion is reduced by giving the maximum safe volume of a special red cell component with a high haematocrit (Table 10.1). Transfusion volume is calculated by the fetal medicine specialist using a formula based on the haematocrits of the donor blood and fetus, the estimated feto-placental blood volume and the target haematocrit. The component is warmed to 37°C immediately before transfusion. Whenever possible, red cells for IUT are requested well in advance of the planned transfusion, in close communication with the Blood Services. In extreme emergencies, where delay in obtaining special IUT blood would be life-threatening, blood from a neonatal exchange transfusion unit or paedipack should be used (irradiated if time allows, but not maternal blood). The SHOT Annual Report 2012 included a neonatal death from transfusion-associated graft-versus-host disease (TA-GvHD) when non-irradiated non-leucodepleted maternal red cells were used for an urgent IUT (http://www.shotuk.org/shot-reports/report-summary-and-supplement-2012/). Babies who have received IUT should be transfused with irradiated cellular blood components until 6 months of post-gestational age.

### Table 10.1  Red cell component for IUT

Plasma reduced (haematocrit 0.7–0.85)

In citrate phosphate dextrose (CPD) anticoagulant (theoretical risk of toxicity from additive solutions)

Leucocyte-depleted

Less than 5 days old (to avoid hyperkalaemia)

Cytomegalovirus (CMV) antibody negative

Sickle screen negative

Irradiated to prevent TA-GvHD (shelf life 24 hours)

Usually group O with low-titre haemolysins (or ABO identical with the fetus)

RhD and Kell negative and red cell antigen negative for maternal alloantibodies

Indirect antiglobulin test (IAT) crossmatch compatible with the mother's plasma

## 10.1.2  Intrauterine transfusion of platelets and management of NAIT

The IUT of platelets is used in the treatment of severe fetal thrombocytopenia due to platelet alloimmunisation (neonatal alloimmune thrombocytopenia – NAIT). NAIT is the platelet equivalent of HDFN. Maternal alloantibodies to antigens on fetal platelets cause fetal and/or neonatal thrombocytopenia with a high (10%) risk of intracerebral haemorrhage. Nearly all cases are caused by antibodies to HPA-1a (80–90% of cases), HPA-5b or HPA-3a. The mother is negative for the implicated platelet antigen and NAIT is diagnosed by demonstrating the platelet alloantibody in maternal serum. The diagnosis is most often made when an otherwise healthy neonate presents with purpura and an isolated severe thrombocytopenia. Subsequent 'at risk' pregnancies should be managed in a fetal medicine centre as prenatal management is rapidly evolving (Peterson et al., 2013 (http://www.ncbi.nlm.nih.gov/pubmed/23384054)). Management is influenced by any history of previous fetal losses and their timing. Fetal blood sampling and platelet transfusion carry a significant risk of life-threatening haemorrhage (suitable platelets should always be immediately available when fetal blood sampling is performed). There is an increasing trend to use a non-invasive approach with maternal intravenous immunoglobulin and steroids and to avoid fetal transfusion where possible. Hyperconcentrated platelets for IUT are specially prepared by the Blood Services (see Table 10.2) and transfusion should be planned in advance. The transfusion volume is determined from the fetal and platelet concentrate platelet count and estimated feto-placental volume. Platelets are transfused more slowly than IUT red cells because of a risk of fetal stroke.

10 Effective transfusion in paediatric practice

**Table 10.2 Platelets for intrauterine transfusion**

| |
|---|
| HPA-compatible with maternal alloantibody |
| Hyperconcentrated to at least $2000 \times 10^9$/L |
| Irradiated |
| CMV negative |

Neonates with suspected or proven NAIT who are severely thrombocytopenic (<$30 \times 10^9$/L) should be transfused with HPA-compatible platelets. HPA1a/5b negative platelet units are usually available 'off the shelf' from the Blood Services. Neonates with intracranial haemorrhage (ICH) or a previous affected sibling with ICH are transfused at a threshold of $50 \times 10^9$/L. If HPA-compatible platelets are not available in a clinically relevant time frame, random donor neonatal platelets should be transfused and will produce a temporary platelet increment in most cases. Spontaneous recovery of the platelet count usually occurs within 1 to 6 weeks as maternally derived antibody levels fall. For babies with persistent severe thrombocytopenia, intravenous immunoglobulin improves the count in around 75% of cases, but response is often delayed for 24–48 hours.

# 10.2 Neonatal transfusion

Neonates are defined as infants up to 28 days after birth. Most neonatal transfusions are carried out in low birth weight preterm infants treated on neonatal intensive care units (NICUs). Transfusion triggers in neonates are controversial and mainly based on expert clinical opinion, although recent randomised controlled trials of 'liberal' versus 'restrictive' red cell transfusion policies in very low birth weight preterm babies are starting to influence clinical guidelines.

## 10.2.1 Neonatal red cell exchange transfusion

Neonatal red cell exchange transfusion is mainly used in the treatment of severe hyperbilirubinaemia or anaemia in babies with HDFN. It removes antibody-coated neonatal red cells and reduces the level of plasma unconjugated bilirubin (the cause of bilirubin encephalopathy). The steep decline in the incidence of HDFN following the introduction of maternal anti-D Ig prophylaxis, more effective antenatal monitoring and treatment, and the use of intensive phototherapy and intravenous immunoglobulin postnatally has made red cell exchange transfusion an uncommon procedure that should only be performed in specialist units by experienced staff. A 'double volume exchange' (160–200 mL/kg) removes around 90% of neonatal red cells and 50% of bilirubin.

The Blood Services produce a special red cell component for neonatal exchange transfusion (Table 10.3). It is ordered in specially by hospitals when required and close collaboration between the clinical team, hospital transfusion laboratory and blood service is essential. The component should be warmed to 37°C immediately before transfusion. It should be irradiated if this requirement does not cause clinically important delay in provision (irradiation is essential if the baby has received IUT).

### Table 10.3  Red cells for neonatal exchange transfusion

Plasma reduced with haematocrit of 0.5–0.6 (NHSBT 0.5–0.55) to reduce the risk of post-exchange polycythaemia

In CPD anticoagulant

Less than 5 days old

Irradiated (essential if previous IUT)

CMV negative

Sickle screen negative

Usually produced as group O (with low-titre haemolysins)

RhD negative (or RhD identical with neonate) and Kell negative

Red cell antigen negative for maternal alloantibodies

IAT crossmatch compatible with maternal plasma

## 10.2.2  Large volume neonatal red cell transfusion

Large-volume transfusion, equivalent to a single circulating blood volume (approximately 80 mL/kg), is mainly used in neonatal cardiac surgery. The component supplied (mean unit volume 294 mL) is in SAG-M anticoagulant (see Chapter 3) and has the same specification as that used for neonatal 'top-up' transfusions. It should be transfused less than 5 days from donation to reduce the risk of hyperkalaemia. Irradiated blood is required in babies with known or suspected T-cell immunodeficiency, such as DiGeorge syndrome, in which case the blood should be transfused within 24 hours of irradiation.

## 10.2.3  Neonatal 'top-up' transfusion

Repeated small-volume 'top-up' red cell transfusions (up to 20 mL/kg) are commonly carried out in preterm babies, mainly to replace losses from repeated blood testing exacerbated by reduced red cell production ('anaemia of prematurity'). Up to 80% of preterm babies weighing less than 1500 g at birth are transfused at least once. Indications for transfusion in this group have largely been based on the Hb concentration combined with the cardiorespiratory status of the baby (e.g. requirement for oxygen or ventilatory support) and factors such as weight gain, although the evidence base is weak. The new British Committee for Standards in Haematology (BCSH) *Transfusion Guidelines for Neonates and Older Children* (http://www.bcshguidelines.com) suggest the transfusion thresholds summarised in Table 10.4.

### Table 10.4  Summary of BCSH recommendations for neonatal top-up transfusions

| Postnatal age | Suggested transfusion threshold Hb (g/L) | | |
|---|---|---|---|
| | Ventilated | On oxygen/CPAP | Off oxygen |
| First 24 hours | <120 | <120 | <100 |
| ≤Week 1 (days 1–7) | <120 | <100 | <100 |
| Week 2 (days 8–14) | <100 | <95 | <75–85 depending on clinical situation |
| ≥Week 3 (day 15 onwards) | | <85 | |

Several randomised controlled trials have addressed the risks and benefits of liberal or restrictive red cell transfusion policies in very low birth weight infants. A systematic review by the Cochrane Collaboration in 2011 found a modest reduction in exposure to transfusion in the restrictive transfusion groups and no significant difference in mortality, major morbidities or survival without major morbidity. The approximate lower limits used to define a 'restrictive' transfusion policy in these trials are shown in Table 10.5. Although many experts now favour a restrictive transfusion policy (Venkatesh et al., 2013), it is important to note the Cochrane Review comment that 'the safe lower limits for haemoglobin transfusion thresholds remain undefined, and there is still uncertainty regarding the benefits of maintaining a higher level'. Further large clinical trials are advocated, especially to address the issues of longer term (including neurodevelopmental) outcomes and cost-effectiveness. Most local guidelines are closer to the restrictive thresholds used in the trials.

**Table 10.5 Approximate capillary Hb transfusion thresholds used for 'restrictive' transfusion policies in studies evaluated by the Cochrane Review**

| Postnatal age | Respiratory support | No respiratory support |
|---|---|---|
| Week 1 | 115 g/L | 100 g/L |
| Week 2 | 100 g/L | 85 g/L |
| Week 3 | 85 g/L | 75 g/L |

Many neonatal red cell transfusions are given to replace losses from frequent blood sampling. This can be reduced by avoiding non-essential tests, using low-volume sample tubes validated near patient testing, micro-techniques in the laboratory, and non-invasive monitoring where possible. Donor exposure can also be reduced by allocating single donor units, split into 'paedipacks', to babies predicted to need more than one transfusion episode within the expiry date of the donation. This requires close collaboration between the clinical team and blood transfusion laboratory.

The specifications for neonatal/infant small-volume red cells for transfusion are shown in Table 10.6. The typical transfusion volume is 10–20 mL/kg (higher end of dose for severe anaemia or bleeding) administered at 5 mL/kg/h. Top-up transfusions in excess of 20 mL/kg are not recommended because of the risk of transfusion-associated circulatory overload (TACO).

During the first 4 months of life ABO antigens may be poorly expressed on red cells and the corresponding ABO antibodies may not have yet developed (making confirmation by 'reverse grouping' unreliable). Maternal IgG ABO antibodies may be detected in neonatal plasma. Wherever possible, samples from both the mother and infant should be tested for ABO and RhD grouping, an antibody screen should be performed on the larger maternal sample, and a direct antiglobulin test (DAT) on the infant's sample. Because of the significant risk of 'wrong blood in tube' errors due to misidentification, the infant's blood group should be verified on two separate samples (one of which can be a cord blood sample) as recommended for adult patients, providing this does not delay the emergency issue of blood. If there are no atypical maternal antibodies and the infant's DAT is negative, top-up transfusions can be given without further testing during the first 4 months of life. Details of pretransfusion testing in neonates and infants are given in the 2013 BCSH guidelines for pre-transfusion compatibility procedures in blood transfusion laboratories (http://www.bcshguidelines.com). Irradiated neonatal components are indicated if the infant has previously received IUT or has a proven or suspected T-cell immunodeficiency disorder.

**Table 10.6 Red cells for small-volume transfusion of neonates and infants**

| |
|---|
| Haematocrit 0.5–0.7 |
| In SAG-M anticoagulant/additive solution (approximately 20 mL residual plasma) |
| Up to 35 days from donation |
| Group O (or ABO-compatible with baby and mother) and RhD negative (or RhD compatible with the neonate) |
| In practice, many hospitals use O RhD negative |
| CMV seronegative for neonates |

## 10.2.4 Neonatal platelet transfusions

Severe thrombocytopenia ($<50\times10^9$/L) is a common finding in infants treated on NICUs, especially in sick preterm neonates (NAIT is discussed in section 10.1). There is no clear correlation between the severity of thrombocytopenia and major bleeding, such as intraventricular haemorrhage, suggesting other clinical factors are important. Audits show that, contrary to many published guidelines, the majority of platelet transfusions are given as 'prophylaxis' in the absence of bleeding. A randomised trial is comparing transfusion thresholds of 25 and $50\times10^9$/L. Meanwhile, an example of suggested transfusion thresholds is given in Table 10.7. Single donor apheresis platelets manufactured to neonatal specifications are used. They should be CMV-negative and ABO RhD identical or compatible with the recipient. A typical dose is 10–20 mL/kg.

**Table 10.7 Suggested transfusion thresholds for neonatal prophylactic platelet transfusion (excluding NAIT)**

| | |
|---|---|
| Platelets $<20$ or $30\times10^9$/L | In the absence of bleeding |
| Platelets $<50\times10^9$/L | Bleeding, current coagulopathy, planned surgery or exchange transfusion |
| Platelets $<100\times10^9$/L | Major bleeding, major surgery (e.g. neurosurgery) |

## 10.2.5 Neonatal FFP and cryoprecipitate transfusion

Normal neonates have different, age-related values for common coagulation screening tests compared to older children and adults. This complicates the diagnosis of 'coagulopathy'. At birth, vitamin-K-dependent clotting factors are 40–50% of adult levels and are lowest in preterm infants. The prothrombin time (PT), thrombin time (TT) and activated partial thromboplastin time (APTT) may be longer, although overall haemostatic function may be normal. In addition, most laboratories rely on published neonatal reference ranges, which may differ from those using different analysers and reagents. Disseminated intravascular coagulation (DIC) is common in sick neonates and haemorrhagic disease of the newborn due to vitamin K deficiency may cause major bleeding in babies who have not received appropriate vitamin K prophylaxis at birth.

Sick neonates in intensive care are commonly transfused with fresh frozen plasma (FFP), which carries a significant risk of serious acute transfusion reactions (see Chapter 5). The 2009 National Comparative Audit of the use of FFP (http://hospital.blood.co.uk/safe_use/clinical_audit/national_comparative/index.asp) confirmed that, contrary to published guidelines, 42% of FFP transfusions to infants were given 'prophylactically' in the absence of bleeding, on the basis of abnormal clotting tests. BCSH guidelines recommend that FFP should be used for:

- Vitamin K deficiency with bleeding
- DIC with bleeding
- Congenital coagulation factor deficiencies where no factor concentrate is available (Factor V deficiency)

The dose of FFP is usually 12–15 mL/kg. The degree of correction is unpredictable and clotting tests should be repeated after administration.

FFP should not be used as routine prophylaxis against peri/intraventricular haemorrhage in preterm neonates (evidence from a randomised controlled trial), as a volume replacement solution, or just to correct abnormalities of the clotting screen.

Cryoprecipitate is used as a more concentrated source of fibrinogen than FFP and is primarily indicated when the fibrinogen level is <0.8–1.0 g/L in the presence of bleeding from acquired or congenital hypofibrinogenaemia. The usual dose is 5–10 mL/kg.

FFP for neonates (and all patients born on or after 1 January 1996) is imported from countries with a low risk of vCJD and is pathogen-inactivated. Methylene blue inactivation is used by the UK Blood Services and commercial pooled solvent detergent treated FFP is also available. It should be ABO identical with the recipient or group AB (group O FFP should only be given to neonates of group O).

## 10.2.6 Neonatal granulocyte transfusion

There is no conclusive evidence from randomised controlled trials to support the use of granulocyte transfusions in neutropenic, septic neonates. Current guidelines do not recommend their routine use in the absence of further prospective studies.

## 10.2.7 T-antigen activation

Occasional severe haemolytic reactions have been reported in neonates or infants receiving blood or FFP containing anti-T antibodies. The T-antigen may be exposed on the surface of neonatal red cells by neuraminidase-producing bacteria such as *Clostridium* spp., often in association with necrotising enterocolitis (NEC). As T-antigen activation is often found in healthy neonates and severe haemolysis is very rare, the need to screen neonates with NEC and make special components available remains controversial and is not performed in many countries. Red cells in SAG-M, containing only small amounts of plasma, are regarded as safe. All non-essential transfusions of FFP and platelets should be avoided. If low-titre anti-T components are regarded as essential, platelets in platelet suspension medium can be used and methylene blue treated FFP with a low titre of anti-T may be available from the Blood Services.

# 10.3 Transfusion of infants and children

Transfusion is performed much less often in older infants and children. The most commonly transfused groups are children on paediatric intensive care units (PICUs), those undergoing cardiac surgery, transfusion-dependent children with inherited conditions such as thalassaemia major, and those following intensive chemotherapy for haematological malignancy or cancer. Transfusion guidelines and blood components for older children are similar to those for adult patients (see appropriate sections of the handbook). Blood transfusion for children with haemoglobinopathies is covered in Chapter 8.

The dose of blood components for infants and children should always be carefully calculated and prescribed in mL, rather than as 'units' to prevent errors and avoid potentially dangerous circulatory overload. Dedicated paediatric transfusion charts or care pathways can also reduce dosing and administration errors. It is recommended that:

- Red cells are transfused at up to 5 mL/kg/h (unless there is active major bleeding) and the transfusions should be completed within 4 hours (see Chapter 4).
- Apheresis platelets should be used for all children <16 years old to reduce donor exposure. The typical dose for children weighing less than 15 kg is 10–20 mL/kg. Children above 15 kg may receive a single apheresis donation (approximately 300 mL). The recommended rate of administration is 10–20 mL/kg/h. Platelets should be ABO-compatible to reduce the risk of haemolysis caused by donor plasma. RhD negative girls should receive RhD negative platelets if at all possible. If RhD positive platelets have to be given, anti-D immunoglobulin should be administered (a dose of 250 IU intramuscularly or subcutaneously should cover up to five apheresis platelet donations given within a 6-week period).
- FFP should not be administered prophylactically in non-bleeding patients or to 'correct' minor abnormalities of the PT or APTT before invasive procedures. When indicated, a dose of 12–15 mL/kg should be administered at a rate of 10–20 mL/kg/h with careful monitoring for acute transfusion reactions or circulatory overload. FFP should not be used to reverse warfarin anticoagulation unless prothrombin complex concentrate (PCC) is unavailable.

## 10.3.1 Paediatric intensive care

The TRIPICU randomised controlled trial in stable critically ill children by Lacroix *et al.* in 2007 found that a restrictive Hb transfusion trigger (70 g/L) was as safe as a liberal Hb trigger (95 g/L) and was associated with reduced blood use. It remains uncertain whether this can be extrapolated to unstable patients.

Expert opinion now generally favours an Hb transfusion trigger of 70 g/L in stable critically ill children, which is the same as the recommendation for adult patients (see Chapter 7). A higher threshold should be considered if the child has symptomatic anaemia or impaired cardiorespiratory function.

There is little high-grade evidence to underpin guidelines for the administration of platelets and FFP in this group. In general, guidelines developed for adult patients are used (see Chapter 7).

## 10.3.2 Haemato-oncology patients

Children undergoing treatment for malignancy are generally transfused in a similar manner to adult patients. A red cell transfusion trigger of 70 g/L is appropriate for clinically stable patients without active bleeding. Platelet transfusion guidelines are also similar to those developed for adult practice, although a higher rate of bleeding in children with haematological malignancies has been reported. The 2004 BCSH *Transfusion Guidelines for Neonates and Older Children* recommend a standard platelet transfusion threshold of $10 \times 10^9$/L in non-infected, clinically stable children. A threshold of $20 \times 10^9$/L is recommended in the presence of severe mucositis, DIC or anticoagulant therapy. Patients with DIC in association with induction therapy for leukaemia and those with extremely high white cell counts may be transfused at $20–40 \times 10^9$/L and a similar level is appropriate for performance of lumbar puncture or insertion of a central venous line.

# 10.4 Major haemorrhage in infants and children

There is little research evidence to underpin clinical guidelines for the management of children with major haemorrhage. In general, principles developed in adult practice have been extrapolated to the care of children (see Chapter 7). Well-rehearsed local protocols, excellent communication with the transfusion laboratory and involvement of appropriate senior staff with paediatric expertise are important elements of successful care.

Emergency group O RhD negative red cells should be rapidly available, with the option of moving to group-specific blood when the identity of the patient and the blood group have been verified. The transfusion laboratory should be informed of the age and (estimated) weight of the patient to guide selection of appropriate blood components. Age-specific components should be used if available in a clinically relevant time frame. Otherwise, the 'next best' adult component should be used until specialised products are available. Where red cell:FFP transfusion ratios are employed, the ratio should be based on volume (mL), rather than 'units'. Once the patient has been stabilised by 'damage control resuscitation' and transfusion based on clinical signs, appropriate therapeutic targets (based on rapid return laboratory or near-patient testing) are: Hb 80 g/L; fibrinogen >1.0 g/L; PT ratio <1.5; platelet count $>75 \times 10^9$/L.

Based on the CRASH-2 study in adults, the Royal College of Paediatrics and Child Health now recommends the use of tranexamic acid in children after major trauma in a dose of 15 mg/kg (maximum 1 000 mg) infused intravenously over 10 minutes followed by 2 mg/kg/h (maximum 125 mg/h) until bleeding is controlled.

# 11

## THERAPEUTIC APHERESIS

# Essentials

- Therapeutic plasma exchange (TPE) using an automated cell separator removes harmful large molecules, such as antibodies, from the circulation.
- Human albumin (± saline) is the usual replacement fluid.
- Solvent detergent treated fresh frozen plasma should be used for TPE in thrombotic thrombocytopenic purpura.
- TPE is only indicated for conditions where there is good evidence it is effective and the benefits outweigh the risks.
- Therapeutic erythrocytapheresis (replacement of abnormal red cells) is mainly used to treat or prevent complications of sickle cell disease.
- Less commonly used therapeutic apheresis procedures include leucapheresis and plateletpheresis to reduce dangerously high white cell or platelet counts, extracorporeal photopheresis to inactivate T-lymphocytes and column immunoadsorption to remove specific antibodies.

# 11.1 Therapeutic plasma exchange (TPE)

TPE removes large-molecular-weight substances such as harmful antibodies from the plasma. It is usually carried out using an automated blood cell separator to ensure fluid balance and maintain a normal plasma volume. This may require the insertion of a femoral or jugular line to allow adequate blood flow. Typically, 30–40 mL/kg of plasma (1–1.5 plasma volumes) are removed at each procedure and replaced with isotonic 4.5 or 5.0% human albumin solution (some services substitute 25–50% of replacement volume with 0.9% saline). Exchange with fresh frozen plasma (FFP) is reserved for the replacement of ADAMTS13 in thrombotic thrombocytopenic purpura (see below) or to replace clotting factors. A one plasma volume exchange removes about 66% of an intravascular constituent and a two plasma volume exchange approximately 85%. TPE is normally combined with disease modifying treatment, such as immunosuppressive drugs, for the underlying condition.

## 11.1.1 Indications for therapeutic plasma exchange

TPE should only be carried out in conditions where there is good evidence of its effectiveness. The American Society for Apheresis (ASFA – http://www.apheresis.org) produces regularly updated evidence-based guidelines (last updated in 2010). Table 11.1 shows the 2010 category I ASFA indications for TPE (recommended as first-line therapy). Category II indications (TPE is an established second-line therapy) are shown in Table 11.2. The evidence base is constantly developing and the decision to implement a course of TPE will usually involve discussion with a transfusion medicine specialist or other expert from the team providing the therapy.

11 Therapeutic apheresis

Table 11.1 ASFA Category I indications for therapeutic plasma exchange (first-line therapy based on strong research evidence)

| Speciality | Condition |
|---|---|
| Neurology | Acute Guillain–Barré syndrome |
| | Chronic inflammatory demyelinating polyneuropathy |
| | Myasthenia gravis |
| | Polyneuropathy associated with paraproteinaemias |
| | PANDAS[a] |
| Haematology | Thrombotic thrombocytopenic purpura |
| | Atypical haemolytic uraemic syndrome (autoantibody to factor H) |
| | Hyperviscosity syndromes (paraproteinaemias) |
| | Severe/symptomatic cryoglobulinaemia |
| Renal | Goodpasture's syndrome (anti-glomerular basement membrane antibodies) |
| | Antineutrophil cytoplasmic antibody (ANCA)-associated rapidly progressive glomerulonephritis |
| | Recurrent focal segmental glomerular sclerosis |
| | Antibody-mediated renal transplant rejection |
| Metabolic | Familial hypercholesterolaemia (homozygous) |
| | Fulminant Wilson's disease |

[a] Paediatric autoimmune neuropsychiatric disorders associated with streptococcal infection.

## 11.1.2 Risks associated with therapeutic plasma exchange

Plasma exchange with albumin or saline causes a transient fall in blood-clotting factors and mild prolongation of prothrombin and activated partial thromboplastin times recovering in 4 to 24 hours. Clinically significant bleeding is rare but a coagulation screen should be undertaken before surgery or organ biopsy is performed. Other risks include haematomas at venepuncture/line insertion sites, vasovagal episodes with fainting, fluid overload or under-replacement, and allergic or anaphylactic reactions due to plasma infusion.

**Table 11.2 ASFA Category II indications for therapeutic plasma exchange (established second-line therapy)**

| Speciality | Condition |
| --- | --- |
| Neurology | Lambert–Eaton myasthenic syndrome |
| | Acute exacerbation of multiple sclerosis |
| | Chronic focal encephalitis |
| | Neuromyelitis optica |
| Haematology | ABO-incompatible haemopoietic stem cell transplantation |
| | Pure red cell aplasia |
| | Life-threatening cold agglutinin disease |
| | Atypical haemolytic uraemic syndrome (complement factor gene mutations) |
| | Myeloma with cast nephropathy |
| | Red cell alloimmunisation in pregnancy |
| Immunological | Catastrophic antiphospholipid syndrome |
| | Cerebral systemic lupus erythematosus (SLE) |
| Metabolic | Refsum's disease |

### 11.1.3 Thrombotic thrombocytopenic purpura (TTP)

This rare condition is a medical emergency with a mortality of 90% if untreated. It is caused by an acquired (autoimmune) or congenital deficiency of von Willebrand factor cleaving protein (ADAMTS13). TPE, using FFP to replace ADAMTS13, is the treatment of choice and should be started as soon as possible after the diagnosis is suspected, ideally within 4–8 hours. The 2012 British Committee for Standards in Haematology (BCSH) *Guidelines on the Diagnosis and Management of Thrombocytopenic Purpura and other Thrombotic Microangiopathies* (http://www.bcshguidelines.com) recommend solvent detergent treated FFP (SD-FFP) as the replacement fluid. TPE is more effective than FFP transfusion alone. Platelet transfusions are contraindicated in TTP unless there is life-threatening haemorrhage. Thromboprophylaxis with low molecular weight heparin is recommended once the platelet count is $>50\times10^9$/L. Daily TPE is continued until the platelet count has been $>150\times10^9$/L for 2 days.

## 11.2 Therapeutic erythrocytapheresis

Abnormal red cells are removed and replaced by normal red cell components using an automated cell separator. The most common indication is sickle cell disease (see Chapter 8). Side effects from rapid infusion of red cells in citrate anticoagulant include perioral tingling and paraesthesia due to low ionised calcium level.

11 Therapeutic apheresis

## 11.3  Therapeutic leucapheresis

Very high white cell counts in patients with leukaemia can cause life-threatening leucostasis. Removal of white cells by automated apheresis may improve the clinical symptoms until chemotherapy takes effect.

## 11.4  Therapeutic plateletpheresis

This is occasionally used in patients with myeloproliferative disorders and symptomatic thrombocytosis until chemotherapy and/or antiplatelet drug therapy takes effect.

## 11.5  Therapeutic extracorporeal photopheresis

T-lymphocytes separated from the patient's blood are treated with a photosensitising agent, exposed to ultraviolet radiation to inactivate them and then reinfused. Possible indications include graft-versus-host disease after allogeneic haemopoietic stem cell transplantation and cutaneous T-cell lymphoma.

## 11.6  Column immunoadsorption

Plasma is removed by apheresis, passed through an adsorption medium to remove harmful antibodies and reinfused to the patient. Indications include removal of high-titre ABO antibodies before ABO-incompatible renal transplantation.

# 12

## MANAGEMENT OF PATIENTS WHO DO NOT ACCEPT TRANSFUSION

# Essentials

- Respect the values, beliefs and cultural backgrounds of all patients.
- Anxiety about the risks of transfusion can be allayed by frank and sympathetic discussion with a well-informed clinician.
- Blood Transfusion Services provide a range of quality assured information resources for patients, parents and their families.
- Jehovah's Witnesses decline transfusion of specific blood products, usually whole blood and primary blood components. Individuals vary in their choice and it is important to clearly establish the preference of each patient.
- Advance Decision Documents must be respected.
- No one can give consent on behalf of a patient with mental capacity.
- Emergency or critically ill patients with temporary incapacity must be given life-saving transfusion unless there is clear evidence of prior refusal such as a valid Advance Decision Document.
- Where the parents or legal guardians of a child under 16 refuse essential blood transfusion a Specific Issue Order (or national equivalent) can be rapidly obtained from a court.

Every patient has the right to be treated with respect and staff must be sensitive to their individual needs, acknowledging their values, beliefs and cultural background.

Some patients, their family members or friends are very worried about the risks of blood transfusion, especially transfusion-transmitted infection, based on reports in the media or anecdotal experience. Others decline transfusion of certain blood products based on their religious beliefs.

## 12.1  Anxiety about the risks of blood transfusion

A frank and sympathetic discussion with a well-informed doctor, nurse or transfusion practitioner may be successful in allaying concern. Provision of clear, balanced information on the risks and benefits of transfusion and, where appropriate, alternatives to transfusion, is a key component of obtaining informed consent (see Chapter 4). The UK Blood Transfusion Services provide a range of quality assured information resources for patients, parents and their families (http://hospital.blood.co.uk/library/patient_information_leaflets/leaflets/ and http://www.scotblood.co.uk/media/11442/receiving_a_transfusion_v12.pdf).

## 12.2  Jehovah's Witnesses and blood transfusion

Jehovah's Witnesses, with at least 7.5 million active members worldwide and around 130000 in the UK, are the most well-known religious community who decline transfusion of specific blood components. Their decision is not related to perceived risks of transfusion but is a scriptural stand based on biblical texts, such as 'the life of all flesh is the blood thereof: whoever eat it shall be cut off' (Lev. 17:10–16) and 'abstain from the meats offered to idols and from blood' (Acts 15:28–29) (1–3).

Individuals vary in their choice and it is important to clearly establish the preference of each patient.

Nearly all Jehovah's Witnesses refuse transfusions of whole blood (including preoperative autologous donation) and the primary blood components – red cells, platelets, white cells and unfractionated plasma. Many Witnesses accept the transfusion of derivatives of primary blood components such as albumin solutions, cryoprecipitate, clotting factor concentrates (including fibrinogen concentrate) and immunoglobulins. There is usually no objection to intraoperative cell salvage (ICS), apheresis, haemodialysis, cardiac bypass or normovolaemic haemodilution providing the equipment is primed with non-blood fluids. Recombinant products, such as erythropoiesis stimulating agents (e.g. RHuEpo) and granulocyte colony stimulating factors (e.g. G-CSF or GM-CSF) are acceptable, as are pharmacological agents such as intravenous iron or tranexamic acid.

Jehovah's Witnesses frequently carry a signed and witnessed Advance Decision Document listing the blood products and autologous procedures that are, or are not, acceptable to them. A copy of this should be placed in the patient record and the limitations on treatment made clear to all members of the clinical team. It is appropriate to have a frank, confidential discussion with the patient about the potential risks of their decision and the possible alternatives to transfusion, but the freely expressed wish of a competent adult must always be respected. Where appropriate, the patient and clinical team may find it helpful to contact the local Hospital Liaison Committee for Jehovah's Witnesses (contact details should be in the relevant local hospital policy document but can be obtained through the UK central coordinating office, Hospital Information Services – tel 02089062211 [24 hours] or via his@uk.jw.org).

Useful resources to assist in the management of patients who refuse blood transfusions include:

- London Regional Transfusion Committee – *Care Pathways for the Management of Adult Patients Refusing Blood (including Jehovah's Witnesses patients)* – http://www.transfusionguidelines.org.uk/docs/pdfs/rtc-lo_2012_05_jw_policy.pdf
- *Better Blood Transfusion Toolkit – Pre-op Assessment for Jehovah's Witnesses* – http://www.transfusionguidelines.org.uk/index.aspx?Publication=BBT&Section=22&pageid=1352
- The Royal College of Surgeons of England – *Code of Practice for the Surgical Management of Jehovah's Witnesses* – http://www.rcseng.ac.uk/publications/docs/jehovahs_witness.html
- *Developing a Blood Conservation Care Plan for Jehovah's Witness Patients with Malignant Disease* – http://www.transfusionguidelines.org.uk/docs/pdfs/bbt-JW-Care-Plan-Malignant-Disease-2012.pdf

# 12.3 Mental competence and refusal of transfusion

'… an adult (aged 16 or over) has full legal capacity to make decisions for themselves (the right to autonomy) unless it can be shown that they lack capacity to make a decision for themselves at the time the decision needs to be made' (Mental Capacity Act, 2005 [England and Wales]). The legal situation varies slightly between the UK Devolved Authorities, but all specify the tests to be met to define mental incapacity and which individuals or bodies may be appointed as the incapacitated patient's best interests decision maker. No one can give consent on behalf of a patient with mental capacity.

In the case of critically ill patients with temporary incapacity, for example altered consciousness after trauma, clinicians must give life-saving treatment, including blood transfusion, unless there is clear evidence of prior refusal such as an Advance Decision Document. The patient record should document the indication for transfusion and the patient should be informed of the transfusion when mental capacity is regained (and their future wishes should be respected).

Where the parents or legal guardians of a child under 16 refuse blood transfusion (or other medical intervention) that, in the opinion of the treating clinician, is life-saving or essential for the well-being of the child, a Specific Issue Order (or national equivalent) can be rapidly obtained from a court. All hospitals should have policies that describe how to do this, without delay, 24 hours a day.

12 Management of patients who do not accept transfusion

# A

## APPENDICES

# Appendix 1: Key websites and references

## Websites

### UK Blood Services

NHS Blood and Transplant http://www.nhsbt.nhs.uk

Northern Ireland Blood Transfusion Service http://www.nibts.org

Scottish National Blood Transfusion Service http://www.scotblood.co.uk

Welsh Blood Service http://www.welsh-blood.org.uk

### Guidelines and systematic reviews

American Association of Blood Banks (AABB) – technical and clinical guidelines
http://www.aabb.org/resources

British Committee for Standards in Haematology (BCSH)
http://www.bcshguidelines.com

Cochrane Collaboration – systematic reviews
http://www.cochrane.org

NATA (Network for Advancement of Transfusion Alternatives)
http://www.nataonline.com

NICE (National Institute for Health and Care Excellence) – clinical guidelines and quality
standards http://www.nice.org.uk

Oxford Systematic Review Initiative – systematic reviews of clinical trials in transfusion
medicine http://www.ndcls.ox.ac.uk/systematic-review-initiative-sri

Royal College of Obstetricians and Gynaecologists Green Top Guidelines
http://www.rcog.org.uk/guidelines

Scottish Intercollegiate Guidelines Network http://www.sign.ac.uk

Transfusion Evidence Library: systematic reviews and randomised controlled trials
http://www.transfusionevidencelibrary.com

UK Blood Transfusion and Tissue Transplantation Services (professional guidelines, best
practice and clinical information) http://www.transfusionguidelines.org.uk

### Haemovigilance

Serious Hazards of Transfusion (SHOT) http://www.shotuk.org

### Miscellaneous

British National Formulary http://bnf.org/bnf

LearnBloodTransfusion – an interactive e-learning resource for hospital staff
developed by the Better Blood Transfusion Continuing Education Programme
http://www.learnbloodtransfusion.org.uk

National Comparative Audit of Blood Transfusion
http://hospital.blood.co.uk/safe_use/clinical_audit/national_comparative/index.asp

National CJD Research and Surveillance Unit http://www.cjd.ed.ac.uk/index.html

NHSBT Hospitals and Science website http://www.blood.co.uk/hospitals/products

UK Haemophilia Centre Doctors' Organisation http://www.ukhcdo.org

# References

Note: references are cited in the order in which they appear in the text.

## Chapter 1

NHS Blood and Transplant 'Transfusion 10 commandments' bookmark
http://hospital.blood.co.uk/library/pdf/10_commandments_bookmark_2011_07.pdf

## Chapter 2

Milkins C, Berryman J, Cantwell C, Elliott C, Haggas R, Jones J, Rowley M, Williams M, Win N (2012). *Guidelines for Pre-Transfusion Compatibility Procedures in Blood Transfusion Laboratories*. British Committee for Standards in Haematology (http://www.bcshguidelines.com); *Transfusion Medicine* 2013, 23: 3–35.

## Chapter 3

*Guidelines for the Blood Transfusion Services in the UK*, 8th edition (Red Book).
http://www.transfusionguidelines.org.uk/index.aspx?Publication=RB

## Chapter 4

*Guideline on the Administration of Blood Components* (2009). British Committee for Standards in Haematology. http://www.bcshguidelines.com

Green J, Pirie L (2009). *A Framework to Support Nurses and Midwives Making the Clinical Decision and Providing the Written Instruction for Blood Component Transfusion*. http://www.transfusionguidelines.org.uk/docs/pdfs/BTFramework-final010909.pdf

Murphy M, Wallis J, Birchall J (2013). *Indication Codes for Transfusion – An Audit Tool*. http://www.transfusionguidelines.org.uk/docs/pdfs/nbtc_2014_04_recs_indication_codes_2013.pdf

## Chapter 5

Serious Hazards of Transfusion (SHOT) Annual reports and summaries.
http://www.shotuk.org/shot-reports

Medicines and Healthcare Products Regulatory Agency (MHRA), *Serious Adverse Blood Reactions and Events (SABRE)*. http://www.mhra.gov.uk/Safetyinformation/Reportingsafetyproblems/Blood/

Tinegate H, Birchall J, Gray A, Haggas R, Massey E, Norfolk D, Pinchon D, Sewell C, Wells A, Allard S (2012). Guideline on the investigation and management of acute transfusion reactions. Prepared by the BCSH Blood Transfusion Task Force. *British Journal of Haematology* 159: 143–153. http://www.bcshguidelines.com

UK Resuscitation Council (UKRC) Guidelines (2010). http://www.resus.org.uk/pages/guide.htm

Advisory Committee on the Safety of Blood, Tissues and Organs (SaBTO) (2012). *Cytomegalovirus Tested Blood Components – Position Statement*. http://www.dh.gov.uk/ prod_consum_dh/groups/dh_digitalassets/@dh/@en/documents/digitalasset/dh_133086.pdf

## Chapter 6

Boulton FE, James V (2007). Guidelines for policies on alternatives to allogeneic blood transfusion. 1. Predeposit autologous blood donation and transfusion. British Committee for Standards in Haematology (http://www.bcshguidelines.com); *Transfusion Medicine* 17: 354–365.

UK Cell Salvage Action Group (in *Better Blood Transfusion Toolkit*). http://www.transfusionguidelines.org.uk/Index.aspx?Publication=BBT&Section=22&pageid=7507

NICE Clinical Guideline (2005). *Intraoperative Blood Cell Salvage in Obstetrics* (IPG144). http://guidance.nice.org.uk/IPG144

Carless PA, Henry DA, Moxey AJ, O'Connell D, Brown T, Fergusson DA (2010). The Cochrane Library: *Cell Salvage for Minimising Perioperative Allogeneic Blood Transfusion* http://onlinelibrary.wiley.com/doi/10.1002/14651858.CD001888.pub4/abstract

Ker K, Roberts I, Perel P, Murphy M (2012). Effect of tranexamic acid on surgical bleeding: systematic review and cumulative meta-analysis. *British Medical Journal* 344: e3054. http://dx.doi.org/10.1136/bmj.e3054

Shakur H, Roberts I, Bautista R *et al*. (2010). Effects of tranexamic acid on death, vascular occlusive events, and blood transfusion in trauma patients with significant haemorrhage (CRASH-2): a randomised, placebo-controlled trial. *Lancet* 376: 23–32. http://www.ncbi.nlm.nih.gov/pubmed/20554319?dopt=Abstract&access_num= 20554319&link_type=MED

Tranexamic acid for the treatment of postpartum haemorrhage: an international randomised, double blind, placebo controlled trial (WOMAN trial). http://www.thewomantrial.lshtm.ac.uk

Simpson E, Lin Y, Stanworth S, Birchall J, Doree C, Hyde C (2012). The Cochrane Library: *Recombinant Factor VIIa for the Prevention and Treatment of Bleeding in Patients without Haemophilia*. http://onlinelibrary.wiley.com/doi/10.1002/14651858.CD005011.pub4/abstract

## Chapter 7

*Patient Blood Management*
http://www.transfusionguidelines.org.uk/Index.aspx?Publication=NTC&Section= 27&pageid=7728

National Blood Authority, Australia. *Patient Blood Management Guidelines*. http://www.nba.gov.au/guidelines/review.html

Makris M, Van Veen JJ, Tait CR, Mumford AD, Laffan M (2012). Guideline on the management of bleeding in patients on antithrombotic agents. British Committee for Standards in Haematology *British Journal of Haematology* 160: 35–46. http://www.bcshguidelines.com/documents/bleeding_on_antithrombotics_Makris_2012.pdf

Keeling, D, Baglin T, Tait, C, Watson, H, Perry D, Baglin C, Kitchen S, Makris M (2011). *Guideline on Oral Anticoagulation with Warfarin.* British Committee for Standards in Haematology. http://www.bcshguidelines.com

Hébert PC, Wells G, Blajchman MA, Marshall J, Martin C, Pagliarello G, Tweeddale M, Schweitzer I, Yetisir E (1999). A multicenter, randomized, controlled clinical trial of transfusion requirements in critical care. Transfusion Requirements in Critical Care Investigators, Canadian Critical Care Trials Group. *New England Journal of Medicine* 340(6), 409–417. http://www.ncbi.nlm.nih.gov/pubmed/9971864

Retter A, Wyncoll D, Pearse R, Carson D, McKechnie S, Stanworth S, Allard S, Thomas D, Walsh T (2012). Guidelines on the management of anaemia and red cell transfusion in adult critically ill patients. British Committee for Standards in Haematology (http://onlinelibrary.wiley.com/doi/10.1111/bjh.12143/full); *British Journal of Haematology* 2013, 160: 445–464.

UK Blood Transfusion and Tissue Transplantation Services (2012). *Massive Haemorrhage Toolkit.* http://www.transfusionguidelines.org.uk/Index.aspx?pageid=7675&publication=RTC

Association of Anaesthetists of Great Britain and Ireland, 2010. *Blood Transfusion and the Anaesthetist: Management of Massive Haemorrhage.* http://www.aagbi.org/sites/default/files/massive_haemorrhage_2010_0.pdf

NICE Clinical Guideline (2012). *Acute Upper Gastrointestinal Haemorrhage: Management.* Guideline 141. http://www.nice.org.uk/nicemedia/live/13762/59549/59549.pdf

Shakur H, Roberts I, Bautista R *et al.* (2010). Effects of tranexamic acid on death, vascular occlusive events, and blood transfusion in trauma patients with significant haemorrhage (CRASH-2): a randomised, placebo-controlled trial. *Lancet* 376: 23–32. http://www.ncbi.nlm.nih.gov/pubmed/20554319?dopt=Abstract&access_num=20554319&link_type=MED

Villanueva C, Colomo A, Bosch A *et al.* (2013). Transfusion strategies for acute upper gastrointestinal haemorrhage. *New England Journal of Medicine* 368, 11–21. http://www.nejm.org/doi/full/10.1056/NEJMx130015

TRIGGER (transfusion in gastrointestinal bleeding) trial. http://www.nhsbt.nhs.uk/trigger

# Chapter 8

Murphy MF, Waters JH, Wood EM, Yazer MH (2013). Transfusing blood safely and appropriately. *British Medical Journal* 347, f4303.

National Comparative Audit of Blood Transfusion (2011). *Audit of Use of Blood in Adult Medical Patients – Part 1* http://hospital.blood.co.uk/library/pdf/Medical_Use_Audit_Part_1_Report.pdf

Rizzo JD, Brouwers M, Hurley P *et al.* (2010). ASCO–ASH clinical practice guideline update on the use of epoetin and darbepoetin in adult patients with cancer. *Journal of Clinical Oncology* 28: 4996–5010. http://www.asco.org/institute-quality/asco-ash-clinical-practice-guideline-update-use-epoetin-and-darbepoetin-adult

UK Thalassaemia Society. *Standards for the Clinical Care of Children and Adults with Thalassaemia in the UK.* http://www.hbpinfo.com/ukts-standards-2008.pdf

NHS Sickle Cell and Thalassaemia Screening Programme. http://sct.screening.nhs.uk/cms.php?folder=2493

Sickle Cell Society (2013). Standards for the clinical care of adults with sickle cell disease in the UK. http://www.sicklecellsociety.org/app/webroot/files/files/CareBook.pdf

Stanworth SJ, Estcourt LJ, Powter G et al. (2013). A no-prophylaxis platelet-transfusion strategy for hematologic cancers (TOPPS trial). *New England Journal of Medicine* 368: 1771–1780.

Treleaven J, Gennery A, Marsh J, Norfolk D, Page L, Parker A, Saran F, Thurston F, Webb D (2010). Guidelines on the use of irradiated blood components. British Committee for Standards in Haematology (http://www.bcshguidelines.com); *British Journal of Haematology* 152: 35–51.

## Chapter 9

*UK Guidelines on the Management of Iron Deficiency in Pregnancy* (2011). British Committee for Standards in Haematology. http://www.bcshguidelines.com

Centre for Maternal and Child Enquiries (CMACE). *Saving Mother's Lives. Reviewing Maternal Deaths to Make Motherhood Safer: 2006–2008.* http://onlinelibrary.wiley.com/doi/10.1111/j.1471-0528.2010.02847.x/pdf

Tranexamic acid for the treatment of postpartum haemorrhage: an international randomised, double blind, placebo controlled trial (WOMAN trial). http://www.thewomantrial.lshtm.ac.uk

Royal College of Obstetricians and Gynaecologists (2011). *Postpartum Haemorrhage: Prevention and Management* (Green Top 52). http://www.rcog.org.uk/womens-health/clinical-guidance/prevention-and-management-postpartum-haemorrhage-green-top-52

*Guideline for Blood Grouping and Antibody Testing in Pregnancy* (2006). British Committee for Standards in Haematology (a revised version is in preparation). http://www.bcshguidelines.com/documents/antibody_testing_pregnancy_bcsh_07062006.pdf

*Guidelines for the Use of Prophylactic Anti-D Immunoglobulin* (2006). British Committee for Standards in Haematology (a revised version is in preparation). http://www.bcshguidelines.com/documents/Anti-D_bcsh_07062006.pdf

*Royal College of Obstetricians and Gynaecologists (2011). The Use of Anti-D Immunoglobulin for Rhesus D Prophylaxis (Green Top Guideline No. 22).* http://www.rcog.org.uk/files/rcog-corp/GTG22AntiDJuly2013.pdf

*Guidelines for the Estimation of Fetomaternal Haemorrhage* (2009). British Committee for Standards in Haematology. http://www.bcshguidelines.com

## Chapter 10

National Comparative Audit of Blood Transfusion (2010). *National Comparative Audit of Red Cells in Neonates and Children 2010.* http://hospital.blood.co.uk/library/pdf/NCA_red_cells_neonates_children.pdf

Peterson JA, McFarland JG, Curtis BR, Aster RH (2013). Neonatal alloimmune thrombocytopenia: pathogenesis, diagnosis and management. *British Journal of Haematology* 161: 3–14. http://www.ncbi.nlm.nih.gov/pubmed/23384054

Gibson BES et al. (2004). *Transfusion Guidelines for Neonates and Older Children.* British Committee for Standards in Haematology (http://www.bcshguidelines.com); *British Journal of Haematology* 124: 433–453 (a revised version is in preparation).

Whyte R, Kirpalani H (2011). Low versus high haemoglobin concentration threshold for blood transfusion for preventing morbidity and mortality in very low birth weight infants. *Cochrane Database of Systematic Reviews* CD000512.

Venkatesh V, Khan R, Curley A, New H, Stanworth S (2012). How we decide when a neonate needs a transfusion (http://www.ncbi.nlm.nih.gov/pubmed/23094805); *British Journal of Haematology* 2013, 160: 421–433.

Milkins C, Berryman J, Cantwell C, Elliott C, Haggas R, Jones J, Rowley M, Williams M, Win N (2012). *Guidelines for Pre-Transfusion Compatibility Procedures in Blood Transfusion Laboratories.* British Committee for Standards in Haematology (http://www.bcshguidelines.com); *Transfusion Medicine* 2013, 23: 3–35.

Lacroix, J *et al.* (2007). Transfusion strategies for patients in pediatric intensive care units. *New England Journal of Medicine* 356: 1609–1619.

## Chapter 11

Szczepiorkowski ZM, Winters JL, Bandarenko N *et al.* (2010). Guidelines on the use of therapeutic apheresis in clinical practice – evidence-based approach from the Apheresis Applications Committee of the American Society for Apheresis. *Journal of Clinical Apheresis* 25(3): 83–177. http://www.ncbi.nlm.nih.gov/pubmed/20568098

*Guidelines on the Diagnosis and Management of Thrombocytopenic Purpura and other Thrombotic Microangiopathies* (2012). British Committee for Standards in Haematology. http://www.bcshguidelines.com

## Chapter 12

Information leaflets for patients and parents (NHSBT). http://hospital.blood.co.uk/library/patient_information_leaflets/leaflets/

Information leaflets for patients and parents (SNBTS). http://www.scotblood.co.uk/media/11442/receiving_a_transfusion_v12.pdf

Jehovah's Witnesses Hospital Information Services. his@uk.jw.org

London Regional Transfusion Committee. *Care Pathways for the Management of Adult Patients Refusing Blood (including Jehovah's Witnesses Patients).* http://www.transfusionguidelines.org.uk/docs/pdfs/rtc-lo_2012_05_jw_policy.pdf

Pre-op assessment for Jehovah's witnesses (in *Better Blood Transfusion Toolkit*). http://www.transfusionguidelines.org.uk/index.aspx?Publication=BBT&Section=22&pageid=1352

Royal College of Surgeons of England (2002). *Code of Practice for the Surgical Management of Jehovah's Witnesses.* http://www.rcseng.ac.uk/publications/docs/jehovahs_witness.html

*Developing a Blood Conservation Care Plan for Jehovah's Witness Patients with Malignant Disease* (2012). http://www.transfusionguidelines.org.uk/docs/pdfs/bbt-JW-Care-Plan-Malignant-Disease-2012.pdf

# Appendix 2: Acknowledgements

Thanks are due to the following colleagues who kindly reviewed and commented on draft sections and chapters of the handbook:

| | |
|---|---|
| **Shubha Allard** | Barts and The Royal London Hospitals and NHSBT |
| **Su Brailsford** | NHSBT and Public Health England |
| **Therese Callaghan** | Royal Liverpool University Hospital and NHSBT |
| **Richard Carter** | Hospital Liaison Committee for Jehovah's Witnesses, Leeds |
| **Chris Elliott** | The James Cook University Hospital, Middlesbrough |
| **Rebecca Gerrard** | NHSBT, Liverpool (and her colleagues in the Patient Blood Management Team) |
| **Andrea Harris** | NHSBT, Birmingham |
| **Patricia Hewitt** | NHSBT, Colindale |
| **Catherine Howell** | Chief Nurse of Patient Services, NHSBT |
| **Marina Karakantza** | Leeds Teaching Hospitals and NHSBT |
| **David Keeling** | Oxford University Hospitals |
| **Phil Learoyd** | NHSBT, Leeds (retired) |
| **Brian McLelland** | SNBTS, Edinburgh |
| **Sheila MacLennan** | NHSBT, Leeds |
| **Edwin Massey** | NHSBT, Bristol |
| **Mike Murphy** | Oxford University Hospitals and NHSBT |
| **Sue Murtaugh** | Leeds Teaching Hospitals NHS Trust |
| **Helen New** | St Mary's Hospital, London and NHSBT |
| **Kate Pendry** | Central Manchester University Hospitals and NHSBT |
| **Liz Pirie** | SNBTS, Edinburgh (and the many colleagues who commented on Chapter 4) |
| **Simon Stanworth** | Oxford University Hospitals and NHSBT |
| **Hazel Tinegate** | NHSBT, Newcastle upon Tyne |
| **Paul Wade** | Hospital Information Services for Jehovah's Witnesses, London |
| **Jonathan Wallis** | The Freeman Hospital, Newcastle upon Tyne |
| **Mark Williams** | NHSBT, Leeds |

NHSBT – NHS Blood and Transplant

SNBTS – Scottish National Blood Transfusion Service

# ABBREVIATIONS AND GLOSSARY

# Abbreviations

| | |
|---|---|
| **AABB** | American Association of Blood Banks |
| **ACD** | anaemia of chronic disease |
| **ACE** | angiotensin-converting enzyme |
| **ACS** | acute coronary syndrome |
| **AIDS** | acquired immunodeficiency syndrome |
| **ANH** | acute normovolaemic haemodilution |
| **APTT** | activated partial thromboplastin time |
| **ASFA** | American Society for Apheresis |
| **ATD** | adult therapeutic dose |
| **ATLL** | adult T-cell leukaemia/lymphoma |
| **ATR** | acute transfusion reaction |
| **AUGIB** | acute upper gastrointestinal bleeding |
| **BCSH** | British Committee for Standards in Haematology |
| **BP** | blood pressure |
| **BSE** | bovine spongiform encephalopathy |
| **BSQR** | Blood Safety and Quality Regulations |
| **CJD** | Creutzfeldt–Jakob disease |
| **CKD** | chronic kidney disease |
| **CMV** | cytomegalovirus |
| **CPB** | cardiopulmonary bypass |
| **CPD** | citrate phosphate dextrose |
| **CPOE** | computerised physician order entry |
| **DAT** | direct antiglobulin test |
| **DHTR** | delayed haemolytic transfusion reaction |
| **DIC** | disseminated intravascular coagulation |
| **DNA** | deoxyribonucleic acid |
| **Epo** | erythropoietin |
| **ESA** | erythropoiesis stimulating agent |
| **FFP** | fresh frozen plasma |
| **FMH** | feto-maternal haemorrhage |
| **FNHTR** | febrile non-haemolytic transfusion reaction |
| **G-CSF** | granulocyte colony stimulating factor |

| | |
|---|---|
| **GvHD** | graft-versus-host disease |
| **HAM** | HTLV I related myelopathy |
| **HAS** | human albumin solution |
| **Hb** | haemoglobin |
| **HBsAg** | hepatitis B surface antigen |
| **HBV** | hepatitis B virus |
| **HCV** | hepatitis C virus |
| **HDFN** | haemolytic disease of the fetus and newborn |
| **HHTR** | hyperhaemolytic transfusion reaction |
| **HIT** | heparin-induced thrombocytopenia |
| **HIV** | human immunodeficiency virus |
| **HLA** | human leucocyte antigens |
| **HNA** | human neutrophil antigens |
| **HPA** | human platelet antigen |
| **HPV** | human parvovirus |
| **HRQoL** | health-related quality of life |
| **HSC** | haemopoietic stem cell |
| **HTLV** | human T-cell lymphotropic virus |
| **IAT** | indirect antiglobulin test |
| **ICH** | intracranial haemorrhage |
| **ICS** | intraoperative cell salvage |
| **Ig** | immunoglobulin |
| **IM** | intramuscular |
| **INR** | international normalised ratio |
| **ITP** | idiopathic thrombocytopenic purpura |
| **IUT** | intrauterine blood transfusion |
| **IV** | intravenous |
| **JPAC** | Joint UKBTS Professional Advisory Committee |
| **LDH** | lactate dehydrogenase |
| **LMWH** | low molecular weight heparin |
| **MB** | methylene blue |
| **MCV** | mean cell volume |
| **MHRA** | Medicines and Healthcare Products Regulatory Agency |
| **MSBOS** | maximum surgical blood ordering schedule |

| MSM | men who have sex with men |
|------|------|
| NAIT | neonatal alloimmune thrombocytopenia |
| NATA | Network for Advancement of Transfusion Alternatives |
| NHSBT | National Health Service (NHS) Blood and Transplant |
| NICE | National Institute for Health and Care Excellence |
| NICU | neonatal intensive care unit |
| NPSA | National Patient Safety Agency |
| NSAIDs | non-steroidal anti-inflammatory drugs |
| PAD | predeposit autologous donation |
| PAS | platelet additive solution |
| PBM | patient blood management |
| PCA | patient-controlled analgesia |
| PCC | prothrombin complex concentrate |
| PCS | postoperative cell salvage |
| PI | pathogen inactivation |
| PICC | peripherally inserted central catheter |
| PICU | paediatric intensive care unit |
| POCT | point of care testing |
| PT | prothrombin time |
| PTP | post-transfusion purpura |
| RAADP | routine antenatal anti-D prophylaxis |
| RhD | RhD red cell antigen |
| RNA | ribonucleic acid |
| ROTEM | thromboelastometry |
| RR | respiratory rate |
| SABRE | Serious Adverse Blood Reactions and Events |
| SaBTO | Safety of Blood, Tissues and Organs |
| SAE | serious adverse event |
| SAG-M | saline, adenine, glucose and mannitol |
| SAR | serious adverse reaction |
| SCD | sickle cell disease |
| SD | solvent detergent |
| SHOT | Serious Hazards of Transfusion |
| SNBTS | Scottish National Blood Transfusion Service |

| | |
|---|---|
| **SPC** | Summary of Product Characteristics |
| **TACO** | transfusion-associated circulatory overload |
| **TA-GvHD** | transfusion-associated graft-versus-host disease |
| **TBI** | traumatic brain injury |
| **TCD** | transcranial Doppler |
| **TEG** | thromboelastography |
| **THPO** | thrombopoietin |
| **TPE** | therapeutic plasma exchange |
| **TRALI** | transfusion-related acute lung injury |
| **TRICC** | Transfusion Requirements in Critical Care |
| **TRIPICU** | transfusion strategies for patients in pediatric intensive care units |
| **TT** | thrombin time |
| **TTI** | transfusion-transmitted infection |
| **TTP** | thrombotic thrombocytopenic purpura |
| **UFH** | unfractionated heparin |
| **UKBTS** | United Kingdom Blood Transfusion Services |
| **UKCSAG** | UK Cell Salvage Action Group |
| **UKRC** | UK Resuscitation Council |
| **vCJD** | variant Creutzfeldt–Jakob disease |
| **vWF** | von Willebrand factor |
| **WHO** | World Health Organization |
| **WNV** | West Nile Virus |

# Glossary

| | |
|---|---|
| **additive solution** | Solution designed to maintain viability of cellular components during storage. |
| **adult therapeutic dose (ATD)** | Usually used in reference to platelet transfusions. Refers to the amount usually transfused to an adult in a single dose. |
| **allogeneic blood products** | Blood and blood components collected from an individual and intended for transfusion to another individual, for use in medical devices or as starting material or raw material for manufacturing into medicinal products. |
| **allogeneic donation** | Blood donated by another person. |
| **anti-D immunoglobulin** | Human IgG preparation containing a high level of antibody to the RhD antigen. |
| **apheresis** | A process in which whole blood is collected from a donor and separated into components. Some of these are retained and the remainder is returned to the donor. |
| **artificial colloid solutions** | *See* colloid solutions. |
| **autologous blood transfusion** | Transfusion to an individual of blood collected from him- or herself. |
| **blood component** | A therapeutic constituent of human blood (red cells, white cells, platelets, plasma, cryoprecipitate). |
| **blood establishment** | Organisation responsible for any aspect of the collection and testing of human blood or blood components, whatever their intended purpose, and for their processing, storage and distribution when intended for transfusion. Excludes hospital blood banks (EU Directive 2002/98/EC definition). |
| **blood product** | Any therapeutic product derived from human whole blood or plasma donations. |
| **bovine spongiform encephalopathy (BSE)** | A neurological disease of cattle which is generally thought to have caused the epidemic of vCJD in humans. |
| **buffy coat** | The granulocyte and platelet layer that forms between red cells and plasma when a pack of whole blood is centrifuged under suitable conditions. |
| **citrate phosphate dextrose (CPD)** | An anticoagulant used for the storage of donated blood. |
| **colloid solutions** | Gelatin, dextran, starch preparations (artificial colloids) that are used as plasma expanders. |
| **cryoprecipitate** | Precipitate produced after freezing and thawing fresh frozen plasma to precipitate high-molecular-weight proteins including Factor VIII and fibrinogen. |

| crystalloid solutions | Aqueous solutions of electrolytes, minerals or other water-soluble molecules for intravenous administration. Examples include physiological saline (0.9%) and Ringer's lactate solution. |
|---|---|
| cytomegalovirus (CMV) | A type of herpes virus which is transmissible via transfusion and can cause infection in immunosuppressed patients. |
| direct antiglobulin test (DAT) | Also known as the direct Coombs' test, it is a sensitive method to detect red-cell-bound antibody. |
| electronic issue | A safe and rapid method for issuing compatible blood. Compatible units are selected by laboratory computer without serological crossmatch. |
| epoetin | Approved name for recombinant human erythropoietin. |
| erythropoietin | A hormone produced by the kidney that stimulates red cell production by bone marrow. |
| fresh frozen plasma (FFP) | Plasma that is frozen within a specific time period after collection and stored in the frozen state until thawed for transfusion. |
| graft-versus-host disease (GvHD) | A serious condition in which allogeneic lymphocytes attack the tissues of the individual to whom they have been transplanted or transfused. |
| granulocytes | Phagocytic white blood cells. Therapeutic blood component can be produced by apheresis of a donor or from donor buffy coats. Efficacy is uncertain. |
| haemolytic disease of the fetus and newborn (HDFN) | A condition in which fetal red cells are destroyed by maternal antibody, usually anti-D. |
| haemovigilance | The systematic surveillance of adverse reactions and adverse events related to transfusion. |
| hepatitis B surface antigen (HBsAg) | The presence or absence of this surface antigen is used to determine whether blood is infected with hepatitis B virus. |
| hospital blood bank | Any unit within a hospital which stores and distributes, and may perform compatibility tests on, blood and blood components exclusively for use within hospital facilities, including hospital-based transfusion activities. |
| human parvovirus B19 | A non-enveloped virus transmissible by blood products. May cause transient red cell aplasia in haemolytic anaemias or hydrops fetalis in fetuses. |
| intraoperative cell salvage | The collection and re-infusion of blood spilt during surgery. |
| irradiated (blood component) | Cellular blood component treated with 25 gray (Gy) gamma or X irradiation to inactivate lymphocytes that could cause graft-versus-host disease in a recipient. |
| Kleihauer test | A method for counting fetal cells in maternal blood. |

| | |
|---|---|
| **leucodepleted** | Blood component from which white cells have been removed by filtration or another method. |
| **massive transfusion** | Variously defined as the replacement of one blood volume within 24 hours, or of 50% blood volume loss within 3 hours, or a rate of loss of 150 mL per minute in adults. In children it is usually defined as the loss of one blood volume within 24 hours, or 50% blood volume within 3 hours, or a rate of loss of 2–3 mL/kg per minute. |
| **maximum surgical blood order schedule/surgical blood order (MSBOS/SBO)** | Schedule of the normal quantities of blood ordered by type of surgical procedure, set at hospital level. |
| **methylene blue treated fresh frozen plasma (MB-FFP)** | Pathogen-inactivated single donor component produced from imported plasma. Indicated for all patients born on or after 1 January 1996. |
| **pathogen reduction** | Additional manufacturing step in making blood products, validated to remove or substantially reduce infectivity for infectious agents. Includes light-activated chemicals (e.g. methylene blue, psoralens) and solvent detergent treatment. Some non-enveloped viruses may not be reliably inactivated by current methods. |
| **plasma** | The liquid portion of the blood in which the cells are suspended. Plasma may be separated from the cellular portion of a whole blood collection for therapeutic use as fresh frozen plasma or further processed to cryoprecipitate and cryoprecipitate-depleted plasma for transfusion. It may be used for the manufacture of medicinal products derived from human blood and human plasma, or used in the preparation of pooled platelets, or pooled leucocyte-depleted platelets. It may also be used for resuspension of red cell preparations for exchange transfusion or perinatal transfusion. |
| **plasma derivative** | Licensed pharmaceutical product containing partially purified human plasma protein for therapeutic use. Prepared from pooled human plasma under pharmaceutical manufacturing conditions, e.g. coagulation factors, immunoglobulins, albumin. |
| **platelets, apheresis, leucocyte-depleted** | A concentrated suspension of blood platelets, obtained by apheresis, from which leucocytes are removed. |
| **platelets, recovered, pooled, leucocyte-depleted** | A concentrated suspension of blood platelets, obtained by the processing of whole blood units and pooling the platelets from the units during or after separation, and from which leucocytes are removed. |
| **postoperative cell salvage** | Collection and re-infusion of blood from wound drains. Mainly used in orthopaedic surgery. |
| **post-transfusion purpura (PTP)** | Immunologically mediated thrombocytopenia following transfusion. |

| red cells | In this handbook, the term is used for any red cell component unless otherwise stated. |
|---|---|
| red cells in additive solution | The red cells from a single whole blood donation, with a large proportion of the plasma from the donation removed. A nutrient or preservative solution is added (e.g. SAG-M). |
| routine antenatal anti-D prophylaxis (RAADP) | A programme established to further reduce the incidence of HDFN by administering one or two doses of anti-D Ig in late pregnancy. |
| saline | Sodium chloride intravenous infusion (0.9%). |
| serious adverse event | Any untoward occurrence associated with the collection, testing, processing, storage and distribution of blood or blood components that might lead to death or life-threatening, disabling or incapacitating conditions for patients or which results in, or prolongs, hospitalisation or morbidity. |
| serious adverse reaction | An unintended response in a donor or in a patient associated with the collection or transfusion of blood or blood components that is fatal, life-threatening, disabling, or which results in or prolongs hospitalisation or morbidity. |
| Serious Hazards of Transfusion (SHOT) | UK-wide reporting system for adverse transfusion events and 'near misses'. |
| solvent detergent treated plasma (SD-FFP) | A commercially available pooled plasma product pathogen-inactivated by the solvent detergent method (Octaplas®) |
| thrombocytopenia | An abnormally low platelet count which may indicate a bleeding risk. |
| traceability | The facility to trace each individual unit of blood or blood component derived thereof from the donor to its final destination, whether this is a recipient, a manufacturer of medicinal products or disposal, and vice versa (European Commission Directives on haemovigilance/traceability). |
| tranexamic acid | An antifibrinolytic drug that reduces bleeding and mortality in traumatic haemorrhage and reduces transfusion in a range of surgical procedures. |
| transfusion-associated graft-versus-host disease (TA-GvHD) | A fatal complication of blood transfusion where allogeneic lymphocytes proliferate in the recipient causing severe marrow aplasia. |
| transfusion-related acute lung injury (TRALI) | Acute lung injury within 6 hours of a transfusion (non-cardiogenic pulmonary oedema). |
| United Kingdom Blood Transfusion Services (UKBTS) | This comprises the NHS Blood and Transplant (NHSBT), the Northern Ireland Blood Transfusion Service (NIBTS), the Scottish National Blood Transfusion Service (SNBTS) and the Welsh Blood Service (WBS). |

| | |
|---|---|
| **variant Creutzfeldt–Jakob disease (vCJD)** | A fatal disease which may be transmissible through prions transferred during transfusion of blood products from an infected donor. It is believed to be linked to BSE and affects much younger adults than CJD. |
| **viral inactivation** | *See* pathogen reduction. |
| **whole blood** | Blood collected from a donor before separation into red cells, platelets and plasma. |

**Abbreviations and glossary**

**INDEX**

# Index

Index

163

Index

Index